'Seriously fun!'

THE GUMSHOE SERIES OF ARCHITECTURAL MYSTERIES

All human artefacts are enigmas, some more so than others – not least buildings. The Gumshoe series seeks to mine this inherent sense of ambiguity by writing about architecture like an investigation, its history and theory as mysteries just waiting to be solved. In such a guise, authors take on the role of detective, reopening cold cases, profiling characters, searching for clues, following wrong leads, balancing scientific evidence with intuition while toying with the fictional substance of any interpretation. Compelling in image as much as in word, each successive title will endeavour to examine afresh, and often sideways, a panoply of famous or overlooked buildings, and in the process imbue their historiography with all of the insight, wit, mischief, style and suspense that they can inspire.

Edited by Françoise Fromonot and Thomas Weaver

MYSTERIES OF A COMMUNIST CAVE

MYSTERIES OF A COMMUNIST CAVE

LYTLE SHAW

A GUMSHOE BOOK

PARK BOOKS

‘It is a neo-baroque of imbalance, the structural reflection of a desire that cannot reach its object’.

—Severo Sarduy, *Barroco*, 1974

THE CALL OF THE DOME

A curved glass curtain-wall frames a dome that rises up from a slightly tilted ground plane. When this horizontal surface of poured concrete meets the building's vertical slab it slopes up more dramatically but then stops a couple of feet below the undulating wall, supported not by the ground but by piers or pilotis, just barely visible at its joints. Though the glazed office block may seem to float as a result of this detail, horizontally it remains under the gravitational spell of the dome, whose central, orbital point it partially encloses. Strolling along the curving hallways above, you can feel its centripetal pull. It is the same pull that has drawn you across the place du Colonel Fabien in Paris to investigate this odd architectural cosmology in the first place. What is this

Street view from place du Colonel Fabien, 2020

mysterious ensemble of carefully engineered parts? Where is it from? Where is it going?

The headquarters of the French Communist Party (PCF), by the Brazilian architect Oscar Niemeyer, presents itself as the heir to high modernism – with three of Le Corbusier's 'five points' immediately visible and the other two (a free plan and roof garden) only awaiting closer inspection. At first glance, the language of Niemeyer's building is close enough to Le Corbusier's that one might legitimately wonder why French leftists, who almost without exception hated the Swiss architect, would have felt comfortable selecting Niemeyer for such a commission.[1] Nor is this even the building's main mystery. Stranger still is the problem of developing an architecture to represent the Communist Party in France at this particular juncture – the mid-1960s, when key elements within and around the party had launched a critique of representation, both political and aesthetic, nearly as thoroughgoing and disruptive as that undertaken in the Soviet Union during the emergence of constructivism in the 1920s.

There are many accounts of structuralist Marxism, but none have considered what this might have meant for actual Marxist structures like Niemeyer's building, which was commissioned in 1965, a year after Louis Althusser's most famous critique of theories of representation, 'Marxism and Humanism'. Construction began in 1968, the year of ... 1968, but was paused in 1972, the same year Gilles Deleuze and Félix Guattari published *Anti-Oedipus* and Jean-Luc Godard released

---

Oscar Niemeyer, Rio de Janeiro, 1965

Tout va bien. The building was eventually completed in 1980, as both Britain and the United States began a lurch to the right. Though France soon after elected the socialist François Mitterrand for two consecutive terms, and in this sense held out against the rightwards turn, the rise of Mitterrand's version of socialism also marked the end of the PCF as a major political force. Where might one situate the architectural strategies and ultimate social implications of Niemeyer's elegant building in relation to these dramatic unfoldings in its front yard? This is an investigation into these interrelationships through a single building, studied from a variety of angles, in a range of contexts, all radiating out from the central problem of French theory, structuralist Marxism and leftist theories of representation. Or rather, not radiating out from these, so much as putting the building into dialogue with them.

Niemeyer had been exiled from his home country when a military dictatorship took over Brazil in 1964. He moved to Paris in 1965, his right to remain in France ensured by the personal intervention, we are told, of both Charles de Gaulle and the Minister of Culture, André Malraux.[2] Not only was Niemeyer, as the main

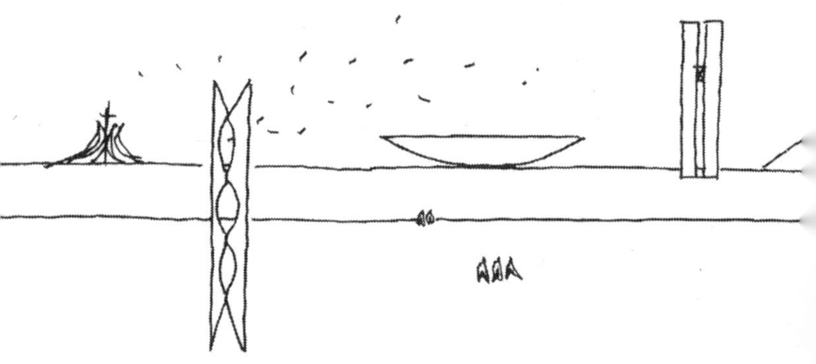

Uma cidade diferente, sem discriminações,
injustiça, opressão e violência, era o que imaginávamos
estar construindo. Antes de 64

Oscar Niemeyer

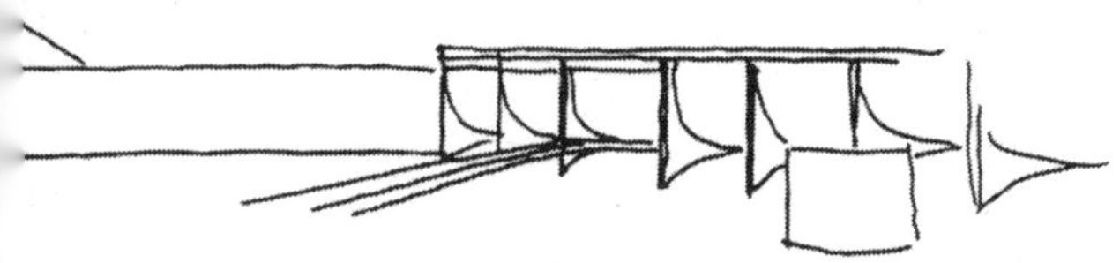

Marcel Gautherot, National Congress Palace under construction, Brasília, 1959 (above); Oscar Niemeyer, sketch of the Palácio do Planalto, Brasília, 1958 (below)

architect of Brasília, responsible for perhaps the most famous large-scale urban architecture of the 1960s; he was also, during the summer of 1965, the subject of an extensive solo exhibition at the Musée des Arts Décoratifs which focused on this nascent city.[3] The exhibition included photographs of both the finished architecture and the ongoing construction process, showing huge cranes hovering over mazes of concrete formwork. Above these were massive reproductions of Niemeyer's sketches – many, like the one showing the curving parallel bars that organise the University of Brasília, reversed out white-on-black. Another wall detailed the structural piers that also operated as *brise-soleils* for the Alvarado Palace. Still another display rendered the symmetrical sinuous ovals of the openings between the vertical concrete pillars of Niemeyer's O Pombal pigeon house on Praça dos Três Poderes into a timeless image of elegance, with flocks of its residents taking to the air in the foreground.

Niemeyer, in other words, had arrived in the French capital as an architectural celebrity and would soon open an office on the Champs-Élysées. But as much

Oscar Niemeyer, University of Constantine campus, Algeria, 1972, photos Michel Moch

as he might have appealed to the French as an exotic genius, exiled by a totalitarian regime, his alliances pointed to the persistence of France's own totalitarianism in the colonies. In Algeria, where the War of Independence had concluded just three years earlier, he had designed a series of buildings (schools in particular) at the behest of the new president. As Niemeyer writes in his memoirs, *The Curves of Time*: 'I am very fond of Algeria. The country's conquest of freedom had brought about a wonderful transformation that I could sense in the euphoria and easy laughter of its people, who had been so horribly oppressed and so dreadfully humiliated.'[4]

The PCF supported anti-colonial revolts as long as they were directed by communist movements. But when they were deemed to have 'bourgeois' roots – as was the case with Algeria's National Liberation Front (FLN) – the party found itself in the uncomfortable position of contesting the path of independence.[5] Niemeyer evidently disagreed with the party's dismissal of the FLN. Describing, retrospectively, his moment of coming to France and designing the PCF headquarters, he stressed how he identified with Jean-Paul Sartre, who famously broke with the party over Hungary in 1956 and Algeria in 1957:

> Those were heady days. I met Jean-Paul Sartre. I thought him extraordinary. Man, cast out into the universe. Meaninglessness, and yet the responsibility that people nonetheless have for each other. An excellent idea... I lived at La Coupole, on the boulevard Raspail. You could meet him there.[6]

Jean-Paul Sartre and Simone de Beauvoir, La Coupole, Paris, 1970, photo Jack Nisberg

'Man, cast out into the universe' – this language of expulsion might at first sound like a generalising reference to existentialism. But the tension between 'meaninglessness' (perhaps the impossibility of fully grounding one's positions) and 'responsibility' pulls this remark back into the domain of the political. In fact, both Sartre and Niemeyer remained committed communists despite the limitations of the actual, official communist parties. Sartre spent the latter part of his life critiquing the machinations of communist parties all over the world and calling for a more liberatory and fair communism. Niemeyer is perhaps aligning himself with this project by mentioning Sartre early in his account of working for the PCF. 'After reading Sartre', Niemeyer continues, 'I viewed life as an unfair and unrelenting tragedy.'[7] That such 'existential' tragedies were political also seems to have been Sartre's suggestion. This was the spirit, then, in which Niemeyer eagerly accepted the commission from the PCF, and in fact designed the headquarters free of charge.[8] A further draw for Niemeyer was undoubtedly that the building was to be situated in a historically working-class, even radical neighbourhood – and one where, just up the street in the parc des Buttes-Chaumont, the Communards had made their last stand.

Niemeyer would speak of the PCF building as 'demonstrating what it was possible to do in contemporary architecture', and even of it becoming a 'tourist attraction'. If tourism was generally frowned upon by the party, it was nonetheless the problem of attracting supporters that prompted the building in the first place. Niemeyer's early sketches stress the undulating ground plane (conceived as extending the public space of the place du Colonel Fabien) and then the primary relation between the magnetic dome and the curtain-wall building that curves toward this source. The suggestion seems

Communard National Guard barricade, Paris, 1871

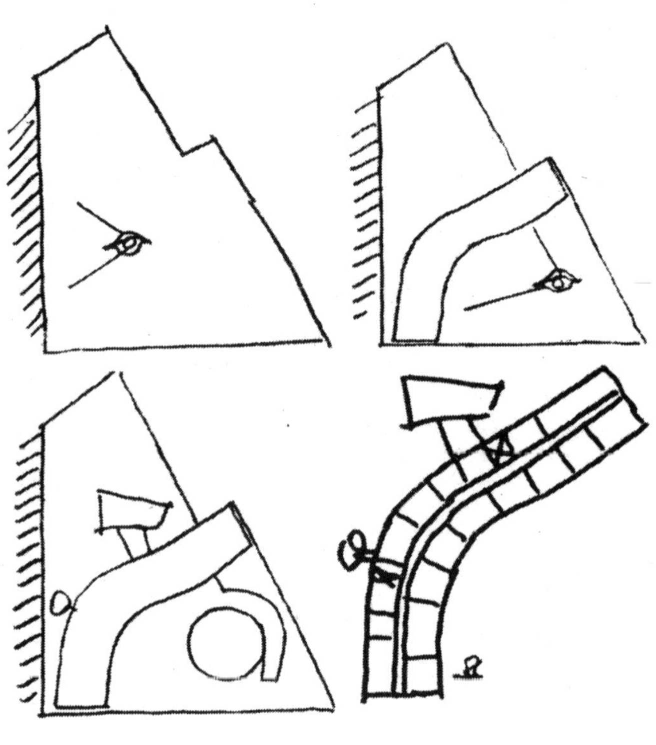

Oscar Niemeyer, schematic design sketches, 1967

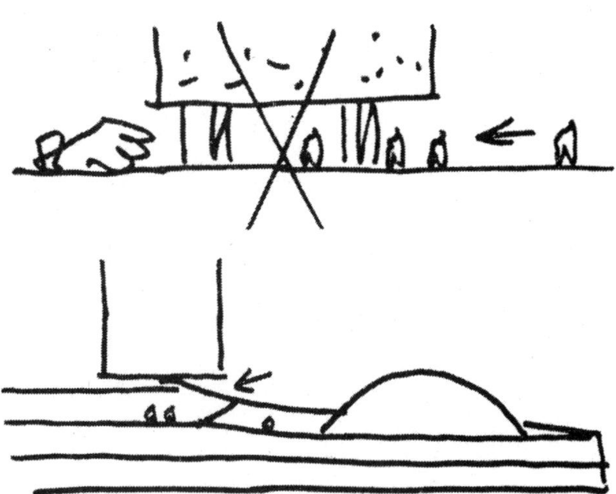

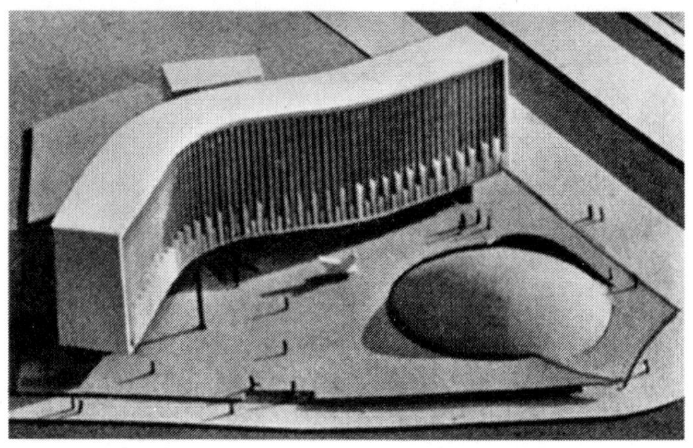

Postcard of an early model of the building, 1968, and (opposite) outline profile of the building's plan imagined as a hammer and sickle

to be that the mass of the sinuous wall is pulled into the orbit of the attractive dome, and that this irresistible force might operate in all directions, including down into the public square. The dome is not entirely surrounded by the curtain-wall. This visual fact makes space for other elements within this orbit – both buildings (institutions) and people (individual subjects) who might begin to feel its pull, visually and politically, and thus come to join the several hundred Marxists already at work within the offices, visible through the glass curtain-wall. At this level, the building might be seen as a neighbourhood-scaled sun designed to attract local heliotropes.

But if the PCF headquarters works at this immediate, physical, almost phenomenological level, perhaps its plan also operates symbolically in a different way. Early responders compared 'the aerial view of the building to the hammer and sickle'.[9] As a simple organising

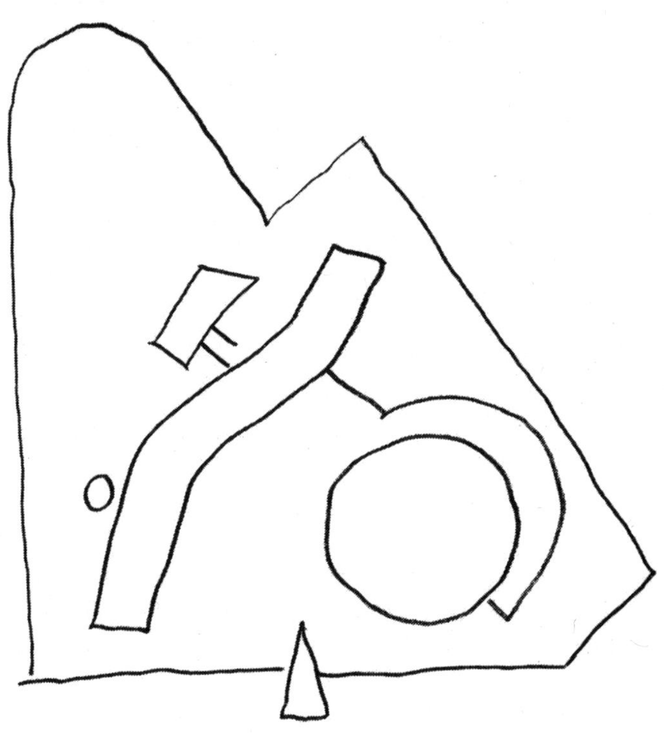

principle for the development of the plan, this would be lamentable kitsch. But abstractions, ambiguities and possible reversals all emerge, suggesting elements in need of adjustment inside the party. For if one initially imagines the two components of party symbolism as indexing a unity, a successful binding together of two domains of production – urban industry (the hammer) and rural agriculture (the sickle) – then the actual history of twentieth-century communism gives us reason to think instead of a never quite reconciled antagonism, which was expressed in diametrically opposite ways in the two largest centres of actual, existing communism. In the Soviet Union, the hammer ruled. Urban industry took the lead and the rural sickle-wielders were always treated as expendable second-class citizens: since their loyalty couldn't really be counted on, they could be worked into the ground when it became necessary for agricultural production to not only feed the USSR's population but also produce a surplus that allowed the Soviet state to buy materials for industrialisation from the West. In Chinese communism, by contrast, the sickle subjects – the rural peasantry – were elevated into the dominant model of virtue, and made the ideological basis of Maoism, with re-education projects always seeking to approximate their supposedly intuitive knowledge of the land, place and production, as yet uncomplicated by elitist, self-interested urban concerns. And so, in China, the hammer was subordinated to and disciplined by the sickle.

In Niemeyer's PCF plan the head of the hammer might be evoked by the crushed rectangle of the circulation tower. But is its shaft the curving bar of the curtain-wall, now rotated 90 degrees and bent? Or is this element just implicit in the line connecting the dome to the bar, while the sickle is in fact the curving curtain-wall bar, flipped around? This basic ambiguity is not easily ironed out. Ultimately, the plan might be taken to evoke the hammer and sickle only if we flip the sickle around in the opposite direction so that it can become the curving curtain-wall. Was this, perhaps, the imaginary reconciliation of these longstanding antagonisms? Or was this an aspirational bringing-into-alignment of the never quite reconciled tensions between the party's two

Oscar Niemeyer and Le Corbusier, among the ten-man board of design consultants, UN headquarters, New York, 1947

populations, and also its two most powerful manifestations of communism, in the Soviet Union and China?

Despite the strong physical and symbolic attractions of Niemeyer's PCF scheme, it is also not entirely clear how the party was able to disentangle Niemeyer from Le Corbusier – who tended to be a focal point of disdain for the French left, from the communists to the situationists.[10] Le Corbusier had, on the one hand, drawn plans for Mussolini, supported Pétain's Vichy regime and worked for a eugenics foundation during the Second World War.[11] But between 1928 and 1932 he had also travelled to the Soviet Union, where he built a headquarters for the Central Union of Consumer Cooperatives and designed a huge (ultimately unbuilt) proposal for the Palace of Soviets. In addition, he built buildings in Algeria and designed the most important precedent for Brasília – the post-colonial government buildings in Chandigarh, India.[12]

Deriving a single and consistent politics from all this is not easy.[13] Even on the most basic level of personal politics, Niemeyer's relationship to Le Corbusier was complex. And beyond this, it was at times difficult to distinguish the particular modernist languages that Le Corbusier developed and Niemeyer widely quoted – so much so that Niemeyer is often simply referred to as 'Corbusian'.[14] If there are ultimately enigmas within Niemeyer's exploration of this language at place du Colonel Fabien, these do not present themselves immediately. Though Niemeyer's more recent reception tends to discuss him in broader, often more South American terms, at the moment of this building, and for quite some time after, his work was not seen to trouble the idea of a Corbusian lineage.

But before we assume that the PCF would necessarily have been looking for a modernist architect, we should remind ourselves of just how recently, and tentatively, the party had turned away from a Stalinist version of socialist realism and back toward the modernism it had abandoned in the 1920s. After support for the party dwindled following the Soviet invasion of Hungary in 1956 – and Khrushchev's revelations about Stalin that same year – modern architecture now seemed to serve the communists' newfound desire to appear more 'open'. According to the PCF dossier, an important factor in choosing Niemeyer was his declaration of 'priorities' ('I have always attributed more importance to my ideological engagement than to my work as an architect') and his impulse toward self-criticism (an expressed dissatisfaction at not being able to work for working-class clients). But since the party's own architects – who had 'monopoly control in the *banlieues rouges* (red suburbs) of Paris'[15] – probably held similar positions, we are left to wonder if the PCF's project of broadcasting openness did not in fact rely on the selection of an international architect. If so, there would have been others worth considering – the rather talented Alvar Aalto is mentioned as a candidate, and other plausible choices could certainly be imagined. Did the fact that Niemeyer had donated the house he owned in Rio (which was then his architecture office) to the Brazilian Communist Party sway things his way? This gesture may have moved some European comrades, but a more likely scenario is that the message of 'openness' sought by the PCF required not just a non-French but a non-European (and yet still evidently modernist) architect.

Oscar Niemeyer at home with his wife Annita Baldo in Rio de Janeiro, 1950, photo Haywood Magee

The architect's status as a Brazilian, then, may well have been the factor that cemented his case. In offering the commission to Niemeyer, the PCF would also have been mindful of the perception of Brazil among its broad support base – some 20 percent of the French populace. This might have been five or six percent down from its peak around the end of the Second World War, but it was still a powerful and popular party, far from merely the ossified domain of doctrine. But what kind of ideas about Brazil did the French population have in 1965, and where had they come from?

Philippe de Brocca, L'Homme de Rio, 1964, and stills (overleaf)

FRANCE'S BRAZIL

Most recently, in 1964, French cinemagoers had flocked to Philippe de Broca's wildly popular *L'Homme de Rio* (*That Man from Rio*), where Jean-Paul Belmondo plays a kind of Indiana Jones *avant la lettre*. The film begins with a man in a dark trench coat stealing an Inca figurine from the Musée de l'Homme in Paris.[1] We later learn that when this sculpture is joined with two others it provides a map to buried treasure. Belmondo is Adrien, an airman with a week's leave to see his sweetheart, Agnès (played by Françoise Dorléac, the sister of Catherine Deneuve). He arrives at her apartment just in time to see her abducted as part of the same heist – she is the key to the location of a second figurine, once

Jean-Paul Belmondo offers an ironic salute, L'Homme de Rio, 1964

owned by her father. Belmondo steals a motorcycle and chases the kidnappers all the way through Paris to the sleek new south terminal of Orly airport (designed by Henri Vicariot and engineered by Jean Prouvé). Fighting his way through the crowds of elegant travellers who stroll in the maze of reflective metal and glass, our hero manages to sneak onto a plane bound for Rio after stealing his ticket from a French general.[2]

Freshly landed in this bewildering metropolis, Belmondo encounters a Brazilian military officer, whom he seems to salute ironically. Was this a jab at the ousting of the democratically elected president, João Goulart – a soldier from a stable democracy behaving irreverently toward a representative of bare military might? No. The film was released more than a month before the Brazilian coup, which began on 31 March. Along with sneaking onto the plane, the gesture thus seems to be part of a more general defiance of military authority.

Niemeyer's move from Rio to Paris the following year can also be understood as an attempt to distance himself from military authority. After the coup d'état, the architect's commissions dried up, his office was raided and, as a communist, his life was at risk. His forced relocation dealt a blow to the country's cultural prestige – he was its most famous architect, and one of its most famous figures overall. And yet at the same time his departure helped fuel his reputation: 'I decided to pack up my architecture and my hurt feelings and go abroad. Those who were trying to blackball me, without realising it, had presented me with the greatest opportunity in my life: to practise my trade as an architect in the Old World and to have them learn to appreciate my nimble forms and curves.'[3]

Oscar Niemeyer at his Casa das Canoas, Rio de Janeiro, 1965

Lúcio Costa, Ministry of Education and Culture, Rio de Janeiro, photo Earl Leaf, 1950

Niemeyer would not build in Brazil again until the transition to democracy was underway in the early 1980s (the dictatorship did not officially end until 1985).[4] Following his return, Niemeyer served as president of the Brazilian Communist Party from 1992 to 1996 – a remarkable role for a world-famous architect then in his mid-eighties, and an extraordinary display of faith after the fall of the Soviet Union, when the prospects for world communism appeared at their bleakest.

In *L'Homme de Rio,* Belmondo's ironic salute seems to give him the confidence to navigate the foreign metropolis. We see him turn toward a clear sign of Brazilian cosmopolitan modernity: a monumental walkway underneath a skyscraper, where the building's pilotis frame a small crowd of passersby who mingle below a modernist mural of organic forms (made by Cândido Portinari). That building, the Ministry of

Education and Culture, is often considered the first modernist building in the Americas. Officially attributed to the architect Lúcio Costa, it was designed in 1935–36 and overseen, if not basically conceived, by Le Corbusier while Niemeyer was an assistant in Costa's office. As Niemeyer himself puts it: 'We have always acknowledged the Ministry of Education design as

Jean-Paul Belmondo in L'Homme de Rio, 1964

Le Corbusier, urban plan for Rio de Janeiro, 1929

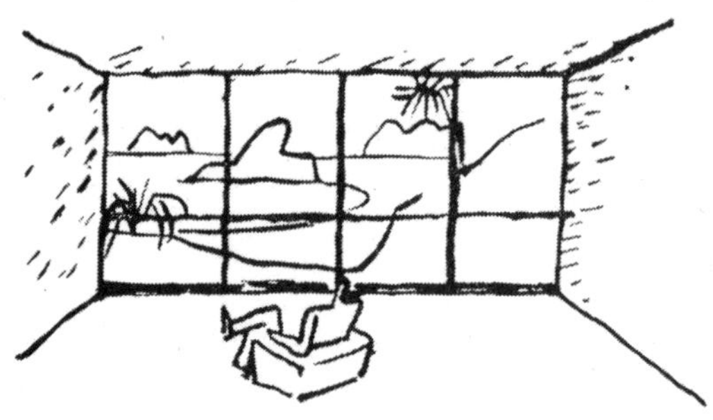

being the work of Le Corbusier. On the commemorative plaque we wrote, "In accordance with the original sketch by Le Corbusier." In architectural vocabulary, the sketch is the original outline, the basic idea, the architectural invention.'[5] Later, though Niemeyer would receive the most international attention for the buildings of Brasília, it was in fact Costa who was in charge of the city's masterplan. And so, the first building we focus on in *L'Homme de Rio* is an instance of European modernism, a tiny relic of cosmopolitan civilisation planted for Belmondo by a fellow European.

And yet, the relationship of influence between Le Corbusier and Brazil appears to have run both ways. As Kenneth Frampton puts it, Le Corbusier's encounter with the Brazilian landscape caused him to 'abandon his ideal utopian urban model because of the obdurate character of the *topos* itself'.[6] Confronted with an extreme terrain that resisted attempts at geometric idealisation, the architect sought instead to learn from 'the narrow volcanic contours of the Rio de Janeiro corniche, which he first experienced when he visited Brazil

Le Corbusier, sketch from La Maison des hommes, 1942

in 1929. He seems to have realised on this occasion that in many instances it would be inappropriate, if not impossible, to impose idealised urban grids on highly contoured, irregular sites.'[7] How consistently this chastening lesson in the de-idealising powers of topography stuck when Le Corbusier was back in the old world is another matter. But that this initial instruction seems to have happened here in Brazil is worth noting. In other words, for the architect Brazil is something more than merely a new context for his influence.

A bit like the diffusion of surrealism in the Caribbean and South and Central America, the idea

Oscar Niemeyer, Henrique Xavier House, Rio de Janeiro, 1936

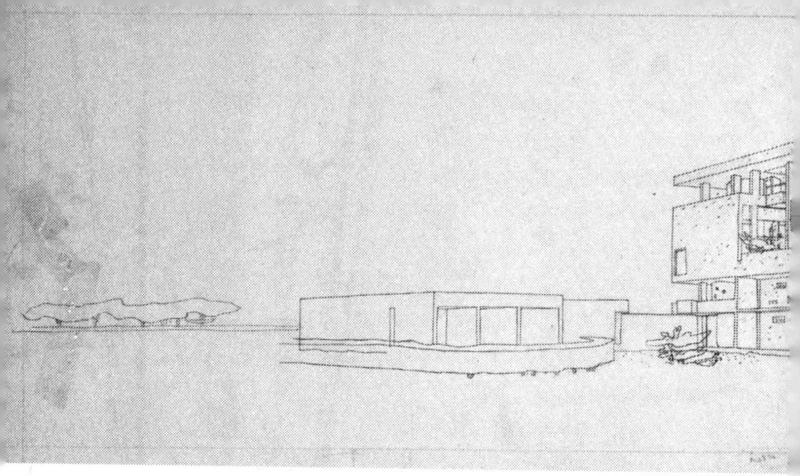

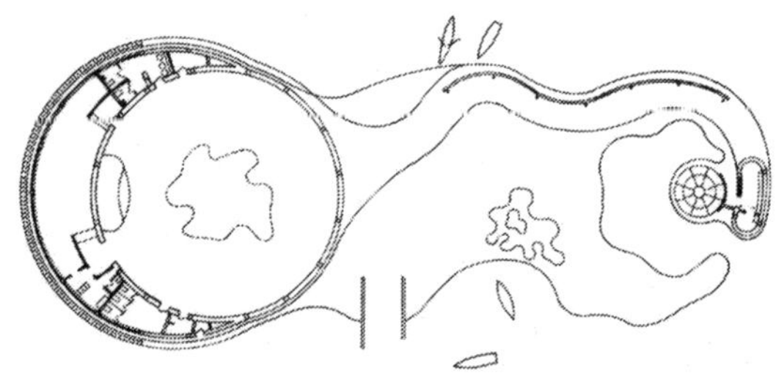

Oscar Niemeyer, yacht club, Belo Horizonte, 1940 (above);
Casa do Baile, Belo Horizonte, 1942 (below)

Le Corbusier, Villa Shodhan, Ahmedabad, 1951

of a cosmopolitan modernism emerging in Brazil, at once European in origin and 'universal', helped to make Niemeyer's early works legible to American and European audiences. Again and again they were framed using Le Corbusier's language, from his Henrique Xavier House in Rio (described in the first monograph on the architect as developing the Corbusian idea of the 'dwelling-tree'[8] and paired with a a later realisation of the same concept in Le Corbusier's Villa Shodhan), through to the buildings realised in Belo Horizonte (which were shown at MoMA in the 1943 'Brazil Builds' exhibition, where again the Swiss-French modernist was the frame), all the way to the most explicit statement of the relation in the 1949 MoMA exhibition, 'From Le Corbusier to Niemeyer'. The press release for this last exhibition suggests that it will 'show the influence of the work of the pioneer Swiss architect, Le Corbusier, on

that of the important Brazilian architect of the younger generation, Oscar Niemeyer'.[9]

Against this backdrop, it is not surprising that *L'Homme de Rio* flashes a cultural Easter egg early on: a European work taken to launch Brazilian modernism, and taken, in the movie, to reassure Belmondo in an alien world. Our hero will need such reassurance as he takes several more wrong turns before he begins to find his way, in large part through the offices of a young parentless bootblack – Sir Winston – who helps him navigate the city, immersing us further in the currents of Brazilian architecture. For though Sir Winston lives in a Rio favela, his home is not just any shack but instead a modernist wonder atop a hillside – a wooden structure suspended on a small metal observation tower, with a Niemeyer-like cantilevered porch and, inside, custom fold-down beds and tables. Sir Winston's preteen bachelor pad acquaints us with a kind of popular modernism supposedly within the means of shoeshine

boys who cannot afford poured concrete slabs and curtain-walls. Soon, however, we will return to official state modernism, since the plot takes us to Brasília. Here, we watch Belmondo get chased through several construction sites, with iconic profiles of Niemeyer's main government buildings always in the background: the twin towers of the National Congress, the dome and inverted dome of the Senate and Chamber of Deputies and a bit of the Planalto Palace. In the film, all of this is presented as the design of Mario De Castro, played by Adolfo Celi, a fictional playboy millionaire architect (and soon-to-be Bond villain), owner of the third and final Inca sculpture, who we first see yelling at construction workers as he hurls obviously inadequate drawings into the air while strutting down an unfinished concrete spiral stairway.[10]

The actual story of the development of Brasília presents a number of complications to the typical

Sir Winston's hilltop shack, L'Homme de Rio, 1964

Stills from L'Homme de Rio, 1964

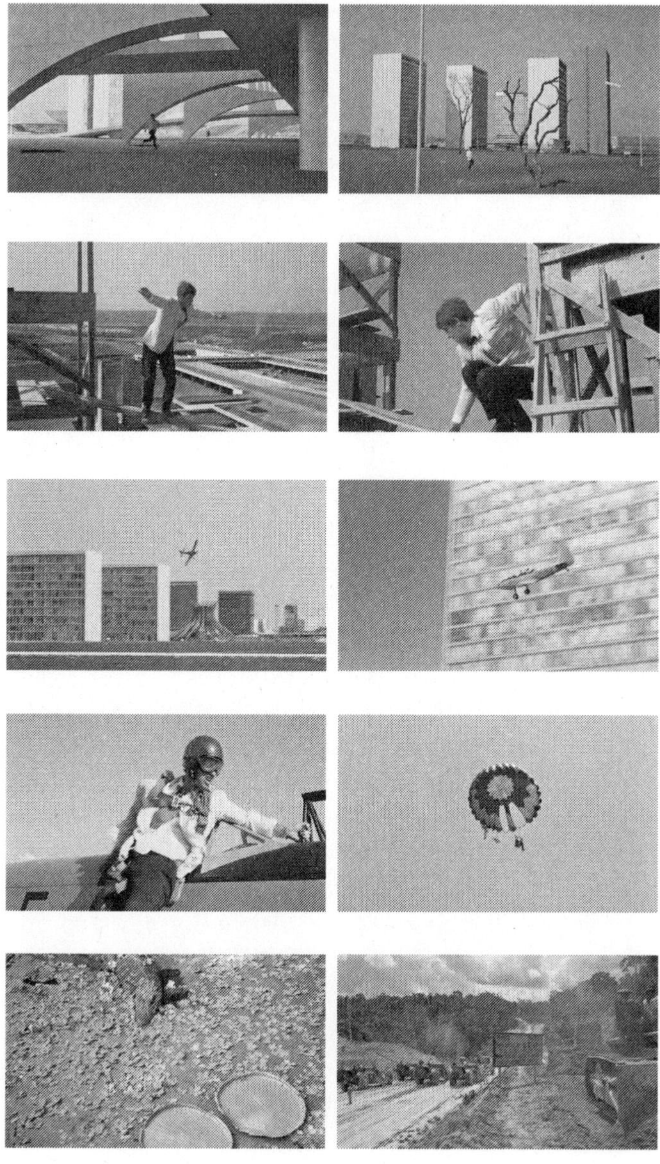

laudatory accounts of the country's new capital. For Brazilian president Juscelino Kubitschek, who initiated the project, and for Niemeyer, too, who designed most of it, the move to Brasília and its fertile interior was understood as a conscious departure from the coastal colonial cities of Rio and São Paulo. In principle, it allowed a wider swath of the population to share the nation's resources, both symbolically and literally, and to rediscover its miraculous landscape.[11] But the reality was much messier. In fact, the native Brazilians who lived on the site that would become Brasília were first displaced, then turned into a workforce that would build the city. They were housed in favelas and bussed into the construction sites, so that their miserable living conditions did not blemish the sleek images of the emerging capital.[12] Despite his own Marxism, Niemeyer tended to look past its favelas and describe Brasília in more heroic terms, though late in his life he was willing to make oblique references to the city's problems.[13]

The architect character in *L'Homme de Rio* – Mario De Castro – is certainly not a friend to the workers or to humanity in general. For a while, we suspect he is the man behind the thefts of the figurines and the larger plot to reunite them – until, that is, he is strangled by the museum curator, Professor Catalan, who turns out to have masterminded the entire criminal undertaking. Now in possession of the third and final sculpture, Catalan rushes off to the Amazon jungle to find the buried treasure (with Belmondo in hot pursuit). But his moment of triumph is short-lived: explosions from the blasting of a highway through the Amazon collapse the mine shaft to his booty and turn the professor, too, into a buried archival relic. Limping back to civilisation after the implausible completion of this Tintin-like escapade, Belmondo passes an Indian family of nine that has apparently been displaced by the same construction process. Modernisation is coming for Brazil and, with it, fundamental change.

The architect-villain, played by Adolfo Celi, in L'Homme de Rio, 1964

What the film cannot add is that this change will be even more disruptive and violent than the process of tearing a modern highway through the jungle with excavators, dump trucks and dynamite. The prime movers in the next phase of Brazil's 'modernisation' will not be construction companies like the Pan-American Highway company, but the military. Along with the Amazonian Palmito trees, large enclaves of leftists will be clear-cut. The road-graders and the helicopters and planes that shuttle construction materials into the forest will be joined by tanks and by death flights that dump abducted Brazilian citizens into the Atlantic. The result will be not just access to the jungle from Rio and São Paulo, but access to, and control of, Brazilian markets by the American companies who were in turn underwritten by *their* military, which oversaw and supported the Brazilian coup.

A month after *L'Homme de Rio* was released in France, just as Brazil's military leaders directed their troops to close in on Rio and take down the democratically elected government, the left-wing president João

Goulart went to Brasília to make a symbolic last stand against the emerging dictatorship. Like Belmondo, Goulart was framing himself against Niemeyer's architectural stage-set of a modern, cosmopolitan and democratic Brazil while being chased by totalitarian thugs bent on eradicating him. Faced with repressive force, Belmondo is able to commandeer planes, jump from automobiles, steal police motorcycles, bicycles and airport baggage trucks, escape from speedboats bent on running him over, parachute out of aircraft and land suspended above alligators, drag himself behind riverboats and ultimately swing from lianas to knock villains into rivers and down precipitous hillsides. Unfortunately, Philippe de Broca was not there to script Goulart's performance.

Final scene from L'Homme de Rio, 1964

President João Goulart makes a last stand outside the National Congress, Brasília, 1964 (top), just before a military takeover of the city and country (bottom)

COMMANDING THE DOME

At the PCF in Paris Niemeyer choreographed his own stunts and distributed them carefully to his leading actors. Though at first glance the star of the show might appear to be the sinuous curtain-wall or tilted ground plane, ultimately this role is reserved for the interior space of the 450-person assembly hall. If the dome is a radiant sun whose light and magnetic force draw in the surroundings, and if the building as a whole is an attractive public heliotrope, the PCF's main hall quietly resists our acquaintance. An otherworldly communist cave – less sticky underground cavern, and more stylish *moderne* grotto – it is accessed through futuristic hydraulic doors whose openings and closings are overseen by a comrade on the far side of a video monitor. Below its anodised aluminium sound diffusers, beneath its curving 11m-high ceiling, this implausible hall presents a glowing galaxy of concentric lights.[1] Outer space has been tactfully nudged underground, where millions of lighted particles create a fluorescent planetarium.[2] Going through the tilted doors, it is easy to imagine this glowing intergalactic cave as a spaceship capable of time travel into any number of communist futures.

Inside, members of the party's central committee lounge on custom red leather chairs at long, curving tables that direct the gaze toward the stage, covered by a thin concrete canopy that appears to have been

---

The ceiling of the subterranean auditorium (overleaf)

Régis Debray, c 1972, photo Louis Monier

peeled back from the cave's wall then folded elegantly and extruded into this partial proscenium. We encounter this sculptural language twice more in the PCF building: first in a similar canopy that hangs over the main entrance, reassuring us as we pass into the underworld; and then, somewhat transformed, in a sculpture of two curving pieces of concrete, the lower one leaning into the upper, which we pass as we walk from the outer gate to the main entrance. Unlike the ground plane – also comprised of concrete that curves near the building – these elements announce themselves as parts of a sculptural programme: a freestanding piece and two focalising devices that guide one into the building and toward the speaker in the assembly hall. Except the speaker would have to be very eloquent to hold our attention in these surroundings. One suspects that the eyes of the audience might turn more easily toward the ceiling. If so, this is a different kind of heliotrope, a fascinating distraction from the business at hand – an architecture temporarily uncoupled from its assumed role as passive backdrop for the making of human history.

Still, the better orators among the committee would have been able to appeal to the shifting yet continually dramatic setting of recent history as the stage for party action. From the end of the Chinese Revolution in 1949 to the Cuban Revolution a decade later, through May 1968, recent history had been dramatic. And if 1968 had failed to establish lasting social change, the prospects for successful revolution in South and Central America still seemed promising – so long as the old formulas of the Russian and Chinese revolts were not blindly applied where they did not fit. This was the thesis, for instance, of *Revolution in the Revolution?* by Régis Debray, a former student of Althusser's. Embraced by Castro and Che Guevara, and published the year Niemeyer began work on the PCF headquarters, in 1967, this manual for contemporary revolution keyed to Latin America adds further heft to the idea that Niemeyer's connection to this South and Central American political landscape of imminent upheavals was a draw for his communist commissioners. This, after all, is where the drama could be found.

Only the drama didn't play out as anticipated. By 1980, the year the assembly hall opened, the whole southern cone of Latin America – some four-fifths of the continent – was ruled by repressive right-wing dictatorships. Closer to home, the crises that had galvanised

SALLE
F

the PCF in the postwar years had dissipated – along with its support base. Despite all this, Niemeyer's faith remained undimmed. When he listed his non-Brazilian buildings, it was usually the PCF headquarters that he mentioned first.[3] He was proud to have realised this particular work in Paris, making his own contribution to the city's vocabulary of modern architecture. But how then are we to understand the fact that all of the building's main elements – the curve of its curtain-wall, the shape of its dome, and even the organisation of its plan – had been used by Niemeyer before? Can we assume that he regarded these elements as tried-and-true 'solutions'? Did their simplicity and elegance recommend them again, despite the different context, despite the fact that the PCF was looking for a new start, a new visual language to signal its relevance and centrality to the contemporary political debate? The last thing the party wanted was to be knowable in advance, pigeonholed into a predictable role. And yet, when we learn that the curve of the PCF's curtain-wall was first used in the Copan building in São Paulo, that the exact shape of the dome was first deployed in the Senate Chamber of the Congress in Brasília, and that even the plan scheme of a curved bar connecting to a dome had a precursor in the Public Library in Belo Horizonte, we might begin to wonder if, in filmic terms, Niemeyer's repeated elements had taken on something of the status of character actors.

To a degree, such actors work their magic because they deliver a similar effect in different contexts.

Copan building, São Paulo (top); Public Library, Belo Horizonte (middle); National Congress, Brasília (bottom)

CNI
EDIFICIO
COPAN

It is unlikely that many Parisians had first-hand experience of Niemeyer's Brazilian buildings, but those who cared about architecture would have recognised his cast of characters since they had seen them often enough in the 1965 exhibition and numerous publications of his work. Should we therefore understand this casting in the PCF headquarters as a conscious decision to cosy the building up to its viewers, to make Marxism seem familiar? Or was the decision less specific and conscious, and perhaps more about Niemeyer's unwavering attachment to his established language, his commitment to the basic vocabulary of his cosmology? If we pursue this latter trail, perhaps the character actor turns out to be the architect himself.

THE ELEMENTARY KINSHIP OF STRUCTURALISTS

'I didn't take leave to play Indian in the Mato Grosso', says Belmondo at one point in *L'Homme de Rio*. The name would have been familiar to many Parisians, who had been learning quite a bit about the Amazonian region from the figurehead of structuralism, whose collection of cultural objects from the Mato Grosso would eventually wind up in the Musée de l'Homme.[1] If structuralism was at the centre of active French intellectual life in 1965, the Brazilian adventures of Claude Lévi-Strauss were arguably its birthing ground. *L'Homme de Rio* mobilises what the French had recently been told about the strange interpenetration of Indigenous new world cultures with

Claude Lévi-Strauss on the bank of the Amazon, Brazil, c 1936

Claude Lévi-Strauss :
Tristes
tropiques

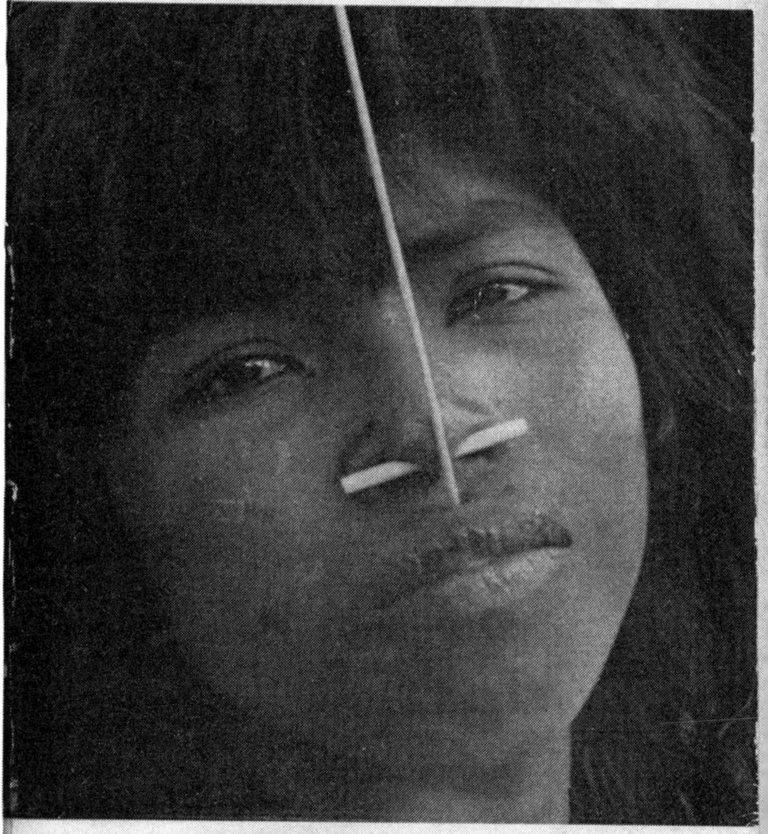

10 18

quotidian Paris: like, who knew that these Indians wore on their faces tattooed images of their impossible-to-realise social aspirations, displayed in paired oppositions? Not as quaint as one might have expected, these pre-modern structuralists! Of course, a Parisian had to go to Brazil to discover all this before these surprising connections could become general 'knowledge'.

That the now omnipotent populariser of structuralism had once been reduced to wandering the Brazilian rainforest, looking for a new field of study, is one of the pathos-inducing undercurrents to *Tristes tropiques* (1955), and part of what makes the book not only a treatise but a memoir, even a kind of *Bildungsroman*.[2]

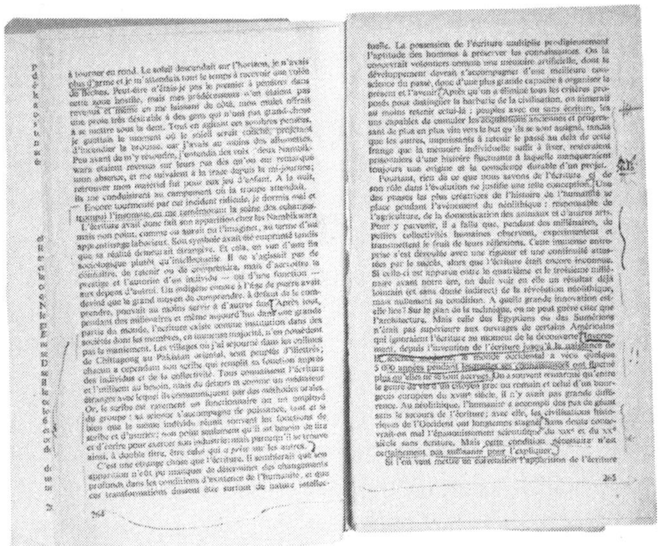

Jacques Derrida's annotated copy of a 1963 paperback edition of Tristes tropiques

When Lévi-Strauss recounts his experiences in the 1930s, he looks back on a period of his own and the profession's adolescence. The anthropologist had been displaced several times, forced to spend much of the war years in exile in the United States, where he finished his first two books (a monograph on the Nambikwara and *Elementary Structures of Kinship*), before returning to France, where he soon became famous. *Tristes tropiques* tries to suggest just how it came to pass that this particular Frenchman was able to write works that changed not only his own field, but also the larger landscape of the humanities. To this end, it offers a tour of Lévi-Strauss's brief sojourns in those other humanistic disciplines and methods he considered studying, but found in one way or another too limited: philosophy, law, psychoanalysis, geology and, not incidentally, Marxism. Extracting what could be salvaged from each, and then reconfiguring this collage of fragments within an expanded and more self-reflexive version of anthropology, Lévi-Strauss narrates the emergence of structuralism.[3] To flip the problem around from the perspective of its setting, we could say that Brazil, in this novelistic tale of French intellectual life, is not just the location for a key breakthrough in one of the main disciplines in the humanities; it is, instead, in the meta-narrative of *Tristes tropiques*, the origin-site for the masterwork of bricolage that will reconfigure all the humanities under the sign of structuralism.

In *L'Homme de Rio*, part of Professor Catalan's evil plan is to suggest that the theft in the Musée de l'Homme has been carried out as an act of revenge by Malket Indians from Brazil. He has his henchman use a poison dart, rather than a traditional slug, to shoot the one guard who, lunch bib still on his neck, had huffed up the stairs to check on the sound of breaking glass. Glossing the Malkets for the benefit of a detective, the professor explains that they were 'Amazonians decimated by the barbarians'. Asked who exactly these barbarians were, he says: 'Conquistadors, Europeans, you, me.' This is, essentially, a popularisation of Lévi-Strauss, who had written:

> The fact is that these primitive people, the briefest contact with whom can sanctify the traveller, these icy summits, deep caverns and impenetrable forests – all of them august settings for noble and profitable revelations – are all, in their different ways, enemies of our society, which pretends to itself that it is investing them with nobility at the very time when

Indigenous Caduveo facial designs from Tristes tropiques, 1955

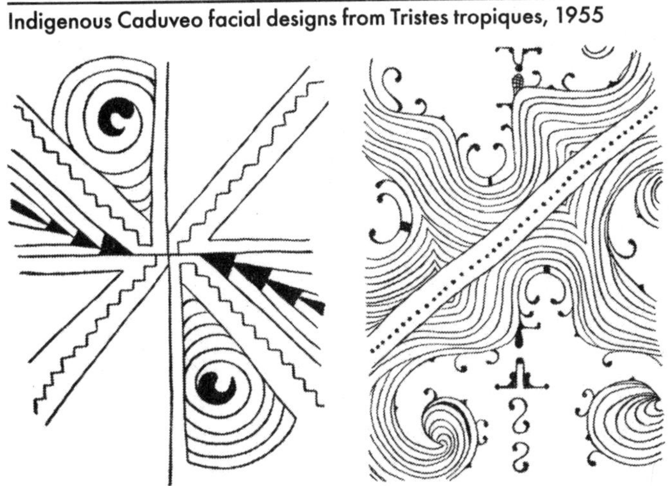

> it is completing their destruction, whereas it viewed them with terror and disgust when they were genuine adversaries.[4]

Like the salute in Rio, the quip about Europeans as barbarians is designed to get a rise out of the French audience: to remind the Parisian cosmopolitans that a few of their extreme eccentrics, including the figurehead of structuralism, might prefer a pre-modern jungle culture to their own. And yet this reference to Parisians' latitude of taste was included to offer itself, at a larger level, as proof of the universal power (and indeed the ultimate superiority) of French culture.

If Lévi-Strauss, deep in the Amazonian jungle, could find that Caduveo face designs were actually structuralist diagrams, perhaps the PCF could also, via Brazil, encounter the Corbusian language of modernism they loved to hate cleansed of its nefarious political associations. Now rising in the strange Brazilian sun, maybe this uncannily familiar architecture might look just different enough that it could be invited back to the capital to represent the PCF in the moment of structuralism – the moment, that is, when the party's relation to its base was itself beginning to look stranger and stranger to Parisian philosophers and aestheticians influenced by the theoretical turn launched by structuralism. Perhaps, then, France did need Brazil in surprisingly important ways: not simply as a primitive foil for its cosmopolitanism, nor as an exotic setting for the discovery of its most cutting-edge intellectual paradigms, but as a discrete wash-house for what it believed was its own slightly soiled architectural modernism.

The simplest objection to this modernism was that it didn't live up to the elegance of the rest of the capital. Parisians could of course afford the luxury of this aesthetic stance because their city had escaped saturation bombing during the Second World War. Consequently, when part of the PCF opened in 1972, modernism was still somewhat uncommon in Paris. Among the most important exceptions were the UNESCO headquarters (1958) in the seventh arrondissement, designed by Bernard Zehrfuss, Marcel Breuer and Pier Luigi Nervi, and Henry Bernard's Maison de la Radio (1963), further along the Seine in the sixteenth.[5] In plan, the UNESCO building is a bent Y-shape that creates three equilateral curving facades covered by *brise-soleils*. Unlike the PCF headquarters, there is thus no distinction between front and back, and no organic blob framed against the backdrop of a facade. As a result, the curving surfaces – seven storeys, raised 5m off the ground by 72 pilotis – operate as sculptural objects as one moves around the building's perimeter. This is perhaps in keeping with UNESCO's more monumental and central position in Paris, sited at the intersection between the two massive formal gardens that organise the west side of the Left Bank near the Seine – the first extending southeast from the Eiffel Tower, the second projecting from the river to the Hôtel des Invalides and the tomb of Napoleon. Maison de la Radio operates in almost the opposite way: here, a basically circular plan comprised of tall curving walls – 500m in circumference – encloses a private courtyard containing a smaller circular building, a tower and a dome. The effect is a bit like that of a modernist castle, a forbidding surface that protects a tower (where radio broadcasts

UNESCO headquarters, Paris (above); Maison du Brésil, Paris, photo Anne Salaün (opposite); Maison de la Radio, Paris (below)

have replaced trebuchet launches) and a mysterious space about which passersby can only speculate.

The city's most famous high modernist works were of a much smaller scale and a bit out of the way. Le Corbusier's Maison La Roche (1925) was tucked into the middle of a somewhat peripheral block in the sixteenth arrondissement; his own house, on rue Nungesser et Coli, was even further out in the sixteenth; while his housing for international students, the Swiss Pavilion (1931) and Maison du Brésil (1957–59), was similarly removed, sitting at the very southern edge of the fourteenth arrondissement, between a pair of large-scale peripheral highways.

It was out here in the Parisian *banlieue*, in fact, that one really saw modernism. And it was here, also, that the further objections to it became a bit more complex. The first, likely to have been heard among Niemeyer's communist clients, was that the country's default architectural language borrowed too much from a goose-stepping Vichy-supporter whose works, in their eagerness to advertise their contemporaneity, often approached a diagrammatic dimension that made actual habitation either generic or unpleasant. This objection could also include the charge that Le Corbusier often bullied his clients into taking up residence inside 'ideas' (demonstrated by his refusal to provide the hostel for the Salvation Army with operable windows) and that he lacked the necessary subtlety to make the adjustments that would allow his concepts to travel, as when, for instance, he gave the Brazilian

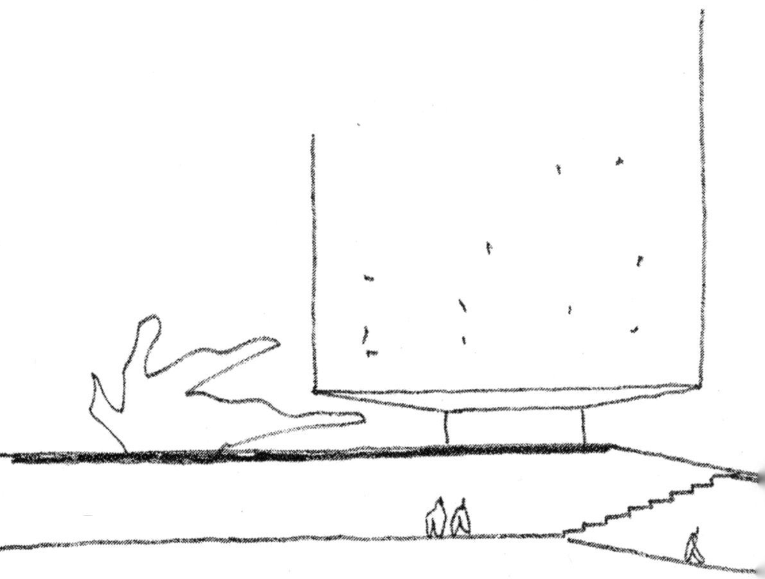

Oscar Niemeyer, sketch section, 1967

House the same kind of Mediterranean *brise-soleils* as his Unité in Marseille. This led to the other main objection to architectural modernism: that the apartment blocks under construction around the whole periphery of the city weren't Corbusian *enough*, and the banal slab buildings – the *Banlunités* constantly pictured in Godard's films from the period – were only cheap and poor imitations of the prototypical housing block in Marseille, with its elegant roof garden, double-storey living units, functional *brise-soleils*, wide hallways, sculptural pilotis and masterfully executed poured concrete elevations. In a weird way, both objections had some legitimacy. But it was the former that was more likely to be heard around place du Colonel Fabien.

Were Niemeyer's clients in the nineteenth arrondissement thinking, perhaps, about their headquarters as a possible response to some of these problems? If the home of Parisian Marxism was going to broadcast its openness by re-embracing modernist architecture and selecting a non-European architect, was it also going to acknowledge the powerful emergence of structuralism in Paris and, increasingly, the world? Were the more intellectually ambitious among these party members

also perhaps speculating about how the increasing prominence of structuralist Marxism might pose new questions for the building of an actual Marxist structure like the one they had just commissioned? Whatever may have been said anecdotally by party members, structuralist Marxism itself, it turns out, did have some basic things to say about architecture.

An architectural problem is at the front and centre of Althusser's attempt to rethink the relation between 'base' and 'superstructure' – between the economic foundation and the political and cultural institutions of a society – in his celebrated 1970 essay, 'Ideology and Ideological State Apparatuses'. Let us investigate these architectonics, however, not through the front gate of Althusser's essay, but instead through the basement of Niemeyer's building – its most ambiguous element. Here, in the dark, we can better pose the question of what it might mean that the 'base' of a Communist Party headquarters is not a solid ground on which the superstructure rises, but instead a hollowed-out warren of underground lobbies, chambers, meeting rooms and assembly halls. For Niemeyer's elegant curving curtain-wall superstructure sits not on an immediately comprehensible support, but on a hard-to-fathom series of pilotis and load-bearing walls that move through the building's lower floors.

As a result, the large proportion of underground rooms presents a basic enigma for interpretation. PCF members may speak proudly of the building's 'transparency' – thinking apparently only of the vertical curtain-wall.[6] But the reality of the entire structure is that much of its programme is stuffed into a series of basement spaces that do not touch the building's exterior. Moreover, one enters the PCF headquarters not by stepping up into the elegant curtain-wall that hangs above the ground, nor through a bright entry vestibule that surveys the surroundings, but instead by plunging into a dark, mysterious gash in the curved concrete and descending into a gloomy green waiting room.

It was perhaps no accident, then, that reviews of the building paused on its entry sequence. Noting that 'Niemeyer did not want this block to sit on stilts inside the usual glazed entrance hall', Sherban Cantacuzino, writing in *The Architectural Review*, proposes that this is what leads to the architect's raising 'the ground level' and bringing 'it almost up to the underside of the first-floor slab, providing an underground foyer large enough for the multifarious activities associated with conferences'.[7] But the critic also suggests that both avoiding a glass lobby and tucking the assembly space underground may have been defensive strategies – anticipations of possible violence not from diehard anti-communists, but from leftists upset about the machinations of the Soviet Union in Eastern Europe: 'Niemeyer's first design was for a *brise-soleil*, demanded, it was said, for security reasons by a client who could not forget the violence of crowds at the time of the Russian invasion of Hungary. Rumour has it that the all-glass facade, substituted at Niemeyer's insistence, is bullet-proof.'[8]

A more sympathetic reviewer for the same journal passes over this proleptical anticipation of violence and sees the structure's organisation as a critique of normative office buildings, a rejection of the sunless, inward-oriented *Bürolandschaft* with its 'soul-destroying spatial

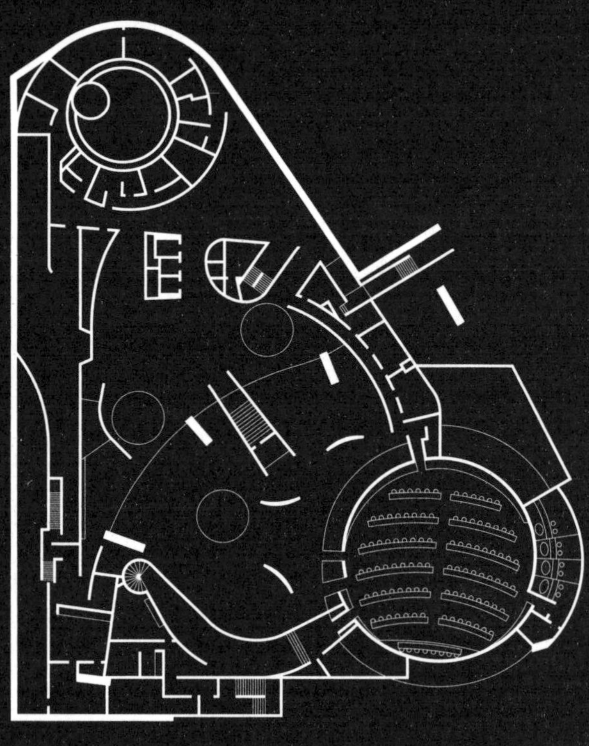

Basement plan with auditorium (left), ground-floor plan, Hôtel de Beauvais, Paris (right)

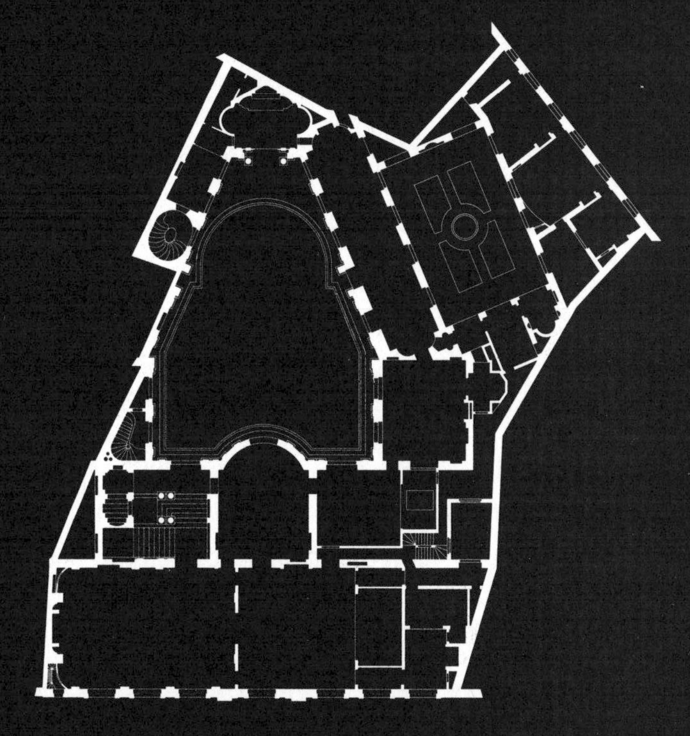

monotony' which deprives 'the individual office worker of any control over his physical environment'. Granting the PCF worker sunlight and the ability, by contrast, to open his window, 'Niemeyer's serpentine slab and Jean Prouvé's curtain-wall ... celebrate the life-giving quality of natural daylight and fresh air, and in doing so fulfil the unwritten part of a brief which called for a didactic building that would serve as an example to the provincial branches of the party and point the way to a brighter future for the working classes'.[9] Like 'transparency', here 'brightness' plays a sneaky double role of linking sunlight with political progress. Luckily, the basement was as yet incomplete.

And yet it was down here, in opaque spaces that did not receive any sunlight or express themselves on the outside of the building, that the central collective events undertaken by the PCF occurred. Given this inward-turning uncoupling from the exterior, the building's lower floors are strangely like another historical Parisian building type: the *hôtel particulier*, the Enlightenment-era urban palaces that, as Michael Dennis has shown, took the irregular perimeters of their sites as givens and then sought to organise these at the level of plan through the imposition of a few idealised forms.[10]

Now for Niemeyer, in his subterranean floors, these idealised forms aren't always quite so ideal: there are some crushed ellipses along with the circles and rectangles that organise his basement plans.[11] Still, the logic is similar, and the resultant space is anything but classically modernist. Niemeyer himself tries to account for the basement as an inevitable solution to the crowding that might have attended more of the building's programme occurring above ground: sinking 'the great workers' hall ... underground allows him to demonstrate the importance of maintaining harmony between volumes and free space on the exterior'.[12] But does the 'freedom' of the plaza really explain the constrained mysteries of the dark basement?

Let us now test this question by sounding these communist caverns. On the first subterranean level we meet an ambiguous series of lobbies, lounges and meeting rooms (all outfitted in green carpet) which surround and serve the domed meeting hall. Mostly deprived of natural light, these spaces are, as the architect's critics have noted, 'rather grim'.[13] True enough, a concrete bank of elevators can take one up into the six floors of offices above, but this ascension to the domain of transparency is not posed as the culmination of the building's circulation sequence; rather, the focal point is the underground cavern – the scene of communist collectivism – which the individual party members will access either directly from the plaza via the descending entry stairs, or by taking the elevator down from their offices to the underground foyer. This shadowy green basement space operates as a kind of architectural hype man for the far more glamorous dome, which one experiences not merely as another room in the compound, but as the mysterious spaceship toward which life in the PCF headquarters has been tending. It seems to have lodged itself into the local geology with some propulsive force, the scene of collision now lit from above by skylights, the dramatic (and only) source of natural illumination in the lobby. This surrounding space does include a few half-hearted attempts at focalisation: a rectangular guards' desk, three circular tables, all of poured concrete,

and a sitting area comprising a table framed by four of Niemeyer's own Alta lounge chairs. But its real role is to underline the dome. Elsewhere on this level, around the edges of the cave's green causeway, snuggled up against the subterranean corners of the building, one finds a warren of meeting rooms with no natural light, again carpet-clad and outfitted with Niemeyer's custom furniture. What sort of topics, one wonders, were reserved for these minor caves? Topics, perhaps, that did not rise to the status of the major cave's tightly managed agenda, but still required underground privacy?

But the mysteries of the communist cave only deepen the further down one goes. Perhaps the most baffling of the floors are the two lowest, which are often not reproduced in publications of the building's plans. These floors are, again, the base of a building designed for the party that theorises the base. In this sense, they have the opportunity to discourse, in some powerful way, on the most fundamental of structural relationships in which one part of society enables another. What, then, is enabled and encountered here? The answer, in short, is automobiles.

These floors are parking lots. This might seem unremarkable, were cars not (at the moment of the building's creation, if not also now) perhaps the most socially charged commodities in the world. Consider, for instance, remarks by Niemeyer's favourite French intellectual, Jean-Paul Sartre, who argued that capitalism not only 'satisfies certain primary needs' but also 'satisfies certain needs which it has artificially created: for instance, the need of a car'.[14] Rather than workers' needs for items like food, clothing and

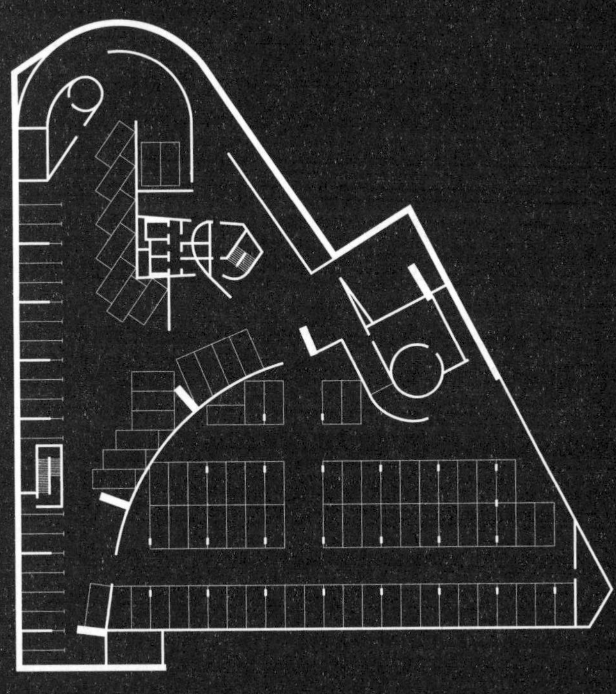

Sub-basement car park plan

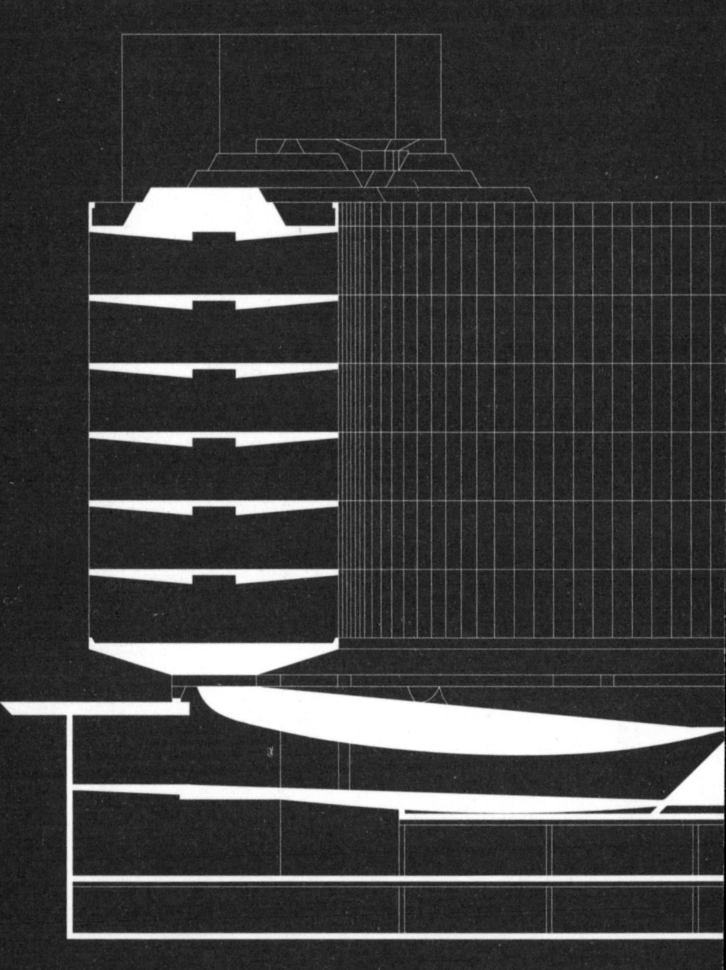

Section through the PCF building, including subterranean auditorium and parking

shelter remaining in conflict with the ultimate operations of capitalism, 'they partly become ... an instrument of integration of the proletariat into processes directed by profit'. After exhausting himself 'in producing a car', the factory worker feels that he has satisfied a 'need' when he has earned 'enough to buy one'. And so 'the system which exploits him provides him simultaneously with a goal and with the possibility of reaching it'.[15]

The PCF was programmatic about resisting American values when it considered its HVAC: air-conditioning would not be automatic and continuous, as it was in the United States, but only used when necessary, and rendered less necessary by the operability of the windows. But when it came to the car, diverging from the US was apparently not a concern. In Sartre's language, a worker is 'serialised' if he is reduced by social forces to an 'atomic', unconnected unit.[16] Workers who do not or

Jacques Tati, Playtime, 1967

cannot bond are serialised. But what was the prospect of each Communist Party member refusing the collective social experience of public transport and arriving at the PCF in his own car – driving one by one down the curving ramp to the parking lot – if not the ultimate image of serialisation? Imagine such a procession of vehicles filmed by Jacques Tati. As we watch the commuting Citroëns descend the curving ramp, each transporting its radical but atomised communist, we would be treated to a special perspective of the PCF building. We are now standing on avenue Mathurin Moreau at the very eastern edge of the site, its highest point.

From here, the building that up till now has presented itself as a curving surface – a curtain-wall framing a sculptural object, a dome – becomes a three-dimensional volume, with the office bar seen in elevation, overhanging the sloping ground. Two narrow car ramps slice into the ground plane, providing the only direct view of the building's communication with the netherworld, which otherwise has to be inferred through its holes in the ground and the dome that bulges out. Here, the office bar also hangs over a narrow causeway that leads from the curving emergency stair (an element that hangs off the building) to an elegant, somewhat diminutive guardhouse that oversees the incoming line of cars. Does a communist traffic officer, whistle on a string around his neck, perhaps step out of this curved structure periodically to impose order over this scene? Because of these two ramps, the sloping mound that has led up to the building is pulled away on the east side, and the elevation is asymmetrical in this regard. A narrow slit of windows at the end of each of the hallways expresses itself in the middle of the bar, which is clad in tile. This is the view from which we are taken as close as we ever get to backstage in the building's composition – the perspective from which we can see the PCF's theatrical gestures without quite being subject to them: its attempt to float above the ground is diagrammatically revealed in the moment the piers touch the earth, and the magical backdrop of the curtain-wall, which again frames the dome, now appears as a weighty volume rather than a dematerialised surface. And yet, even here, the building retains an extremely high degree of elegance. The illusion may be revealed, but we remain just as satisfied by the props and apparatus as we are by the effects they induce.

But now let's poke our heads up from this netherworld and try to grasp the significance of this basement as the physical embodiment of Marxist thinking. If it's a bit strange that a high modernist building becomes something of a *hôtel particulier* below ground, it's stranger still that a Marxist building would pass on the opportunity to emphasise the relationship between base and superstructure. But this is indeed the consequence of hollowing out the basement into a subterranean maze of halls, offices and meeting rooms. It means that one of Marxism's most fundamental metaphoric structures (the metaphor of fundament) is not quite available to it.[17] Yes, all buildings must eventually make connections with a ground plane and yes, the PCF headquarters ultimately rests on the earth. But it does so fully three storeys below the point at which the S-curve curtain-wall meets the surface on which it finally sits. And so, by inverting the programmatic

Louis Althusser, 1978, photo Alain Mingam

requirements and housing the majority of the space in a dark, underground setting, the building not only rejects the rhetoric of transparency but also dispenses with the idea that there is a visible base for the party that theorises the base. Rather than polemically assert, in diagrammatic form, how elegant expressions of culture might rest on the solid footings provided by workers, the weight of the upper storeys at Niemeyer's building dissipates into a bewilderingly shadowy basement – a bottomless cavern of structural mysteries.

GOTHIC OVERDETERMINATION

In 'Ideology and Ideological State Apparatuses' Louis Althusser also considers the illusive concept of base. One might expect, given his rejection of the older division between false consciousness and authentic class consciousness, that he would dismiss outright the traditional language of base and superstructure. But rather than simply sweep it aside, Althusser considers it as preliminary – by which he means the first phase of a theory, which will require the elaboration of his idea of the Ideological State Apparatus (ISA):

> Like every metaphor, this metaphor suggests something, makes something visible. What? Precisely this: that the upper floors could not 'stay up' (in the air) alone, if they did not rest precisely on their base. Thus, the object of the metaphor of the edifice is to represent above all the 'determination in the last instance' by the economic base.[1]

Althusser then overturns previous Marxist thinking and shows the ISA at work within ostensibly private domains. Unlike the repressive state apparatus, however, this apparatus works not through the threat of violence, but through ideology – or rather, through both the power to exert violence and the work of ideology. Here, in contrast to classic Marxist accounts, Althusser is proposing there are two underlying structures – and not just one – that keep any society's upper floors, its culture, from collapsing. This is what he calls overdetermination.

While Althusser's explanation of the function of the ISA does not elaborate on the architectural metaphor, he returns immediately to the idea of building in the postscript to the essay, apologising for what he claims is the still insufficiently concrete character of his analysis: 'If these few schematic theses allow me to illuminate certain aspects of the functioning of the superstructure and its mode of intervention in the Infrastructure, they are obviously *abstract* and necessarily leave several important problems unanswered.'[2] But we perhaps have the opposite problem, for what we turn to next risks seeming ridiculous, not because it is too abstract, but because it is too concrete and too literal.

In the history of architecture, the birth of the gothic was perhaps the classic moment in which the relationship between superstructure and base – between the weight of the building and the elements that support it – underwent a fundamental revision. From the nineteenth century until fairly recently, this was even understood to have occurred in a precise place and time: the renovations undertaken by Abbé Suger at the Church of St Denis in Paris in the 1140s.[3] Even though historians of architecture now see a more complex picture of the emergence of high gothic, one that involves a number of buildings across France, St Denis still remains a key moment in the development of the style.

In earlier Romanesque architecture the primary determinant of base to superstructure had been the

---

Viollet-le-Duc, Basilica of St Denis, Paris, 1860

classic engineering tool of a load-bearing wall. But when this was supplemented with a second kind of support – the gothic flying buttress – it allowed for far stronger, and thus far taller, structures. Rather than operating within the existing plane of the load-bearing wall (as vaulting did), the flying buttress was typically set at right angles to this plane, offering a kind of powerful cross-bracing that could safely transfer the outward thrust of the high vaulted ceilings to the ground. In this way, architectural superstructures redistributed their

Grain silo from Le Corbusier, Vers une architecture, 1923

underlying task of support between two distinct components – walls and buttresses.

But however impressive this team effort might have been, the very fact of two underlying systems was, from the perspective of modern architecture, something of a mystification. Like many rationalist viewers after the Enlightenment, Le Corbusier was not keen on an Aquinas-like account of multiple conditions for the support of buildings. What he wanted was a single, clear and evident structure displayed or, we might say, *revealed* in a building's engineering: 'The primordial physical laws', he cautioned, 'are simple and few in number.'[4] Indeed, it was precisely to bring architecture closer to modern engineering that Le Corbusier launched perhaps the most famous polemic

North elevation of the Basilica of St Denis, Paris

of modern architecture, *Vers une architecture* (1923). 'The Engineer's Aesthetic, and Architecture', he writes in the book's very first sentence, 'are two things that march together and follow one from the other: the one being now at its full height, the other in an unhappy state of retrogression.'[5] To put it another way: engineering projects tend to express not only their functions but also their underlying physical logic, whereas architecture – though likewise reliant on modern engineering techniques – often does not.

As familiar as Le Corbusier's claim might seem in the context of the history of architecture, let us imagine it instead as a reaction against what Althusser would call 'overdetermination', the idea of multiple independent structural systems supporting a building's superstructure. Le Corbusier makes the case for a simpler, more visually satisfying model: 'The Engineer, inspired by the law of Economy and governed by mathematical calculation, puts us in accord with universal law. He achieves harmony.'[6] Explaining how the 'eye observes' the 'comprehensible reasons' that underlie a successful building's structural elements, he proposes: 'The whole structure rises from its base and is developed in accordance with a rule which is written on the ground in the plan.'[7]

In a modernist building you just couldn't have the kind of overdetermination that Althusser talks about. Walls uncouple themselves from structure, become glass and, when they meet the ground plane, do so through a system – here pilotis – that emphasises the engineering that underlies the building. And yet, when one looks closely at Niemeyer's building, its structural mysteries trouble the metaphor of base and superstructure so central to Marxism, both before and after Althusser. By hollowing out the base and developing three huge underground floors, Niemeyer relegates much of the building's programme to a dark netherregion that actively resists the Marxist symbolism of the base we have been exploring. Though we know intellectually that the weight of the upper floors, the superstructure, must transfer itself to the ground somewhere below us, we are not able to experience this, and therefore we are also not able to have the building remind us how the elegant expressions of culture rest on something as primary as labour. At the same time, modernism's typical project of expressing its interior on its exterior also vanishes in this mysterious cave.[8]

These aspects of Niemeyer's design – whether an oversight or interventions – can be seen as a critique of two of the most ossified ideas about the ethical values of architecture: the discussion of transparency that takes place explicitly within the discourse of architecture, and the architectural metaphor of base and superstructure that occurs primarily within Marxist discourse itself. When we link this critique with Niemeyer's larger dismissal of functionalism, and his cultivation instead of a kind of erotics of architecture, we are left with a rather eloquent position statement for a building like the PCF headquarters. The only problem is that its more traditional clients would not have appreciated it. And so, we confront a gap between the building's powerful latencies and the explicit tenor of its tenants, whose pronouncements harped on about values that had long ago left their building.

If the tension between base and superstructure is discussed most explicitly in Marxist writing, other now-canonical leftist architecture from the 1960s addresses the same dialectic. Take, for instance, Dutch artist Constant Nieuwenhuys' New Babylon (1956–74), an imagined space of collective leisure, suspended 15m to 20m above a ground plane and open to continuous, improvisatory rearrangement by its inhabitants, whose only concern is to explore the changing ambiances they create in response to their shifting desires. New Babylon jettisons the hoary concept of base, then, in two fundamental ways. First, as Mark Wigley has suggested, because 'nobody works in this futuristic world'.[9] While this might have been a ridiculous fantasy, it gave rise in New Babylon to a de-solidification of what had been

Constant Nieuwenhuys, Sector Construction New Babylon, 1966

a working-class aesthetic that perhaps parallels Niemeyer. The rejection of labour as a category seems to question both the ontological core of the PCF and the readymade metaphors for any communist building. In this way, Constant's world departs from the base/superstructure model not, as in Althusser, by offering another account of how the superstructure holds. Rather, it simply dispenses with the problem of labour altogether (machines will do it) and offers a monism of superstructure, now imagined as continual leisure in a transformable atmosphere open to any and all improvisatory or emergent desires. Moreover, and this is the second way the project rejects the concept of a base, the literal structure of New Babylon, too, is always lifted off the ground plane, always suspended, always physically superstructural.[10] In this sense, New Babylon's complication of the concept of base is more complete than Niemeyer's.

Now to the problem of transparency, which remains a key term of mystification in architectural discourse, since it is too often assumed that there should be some immediate connection between visual and political transparency.[11] But even if one reasonably rejects this equation, the language of modernism allows for the suggestion that although one cannot actually see into a building one can still have a sense of its discrete parts and their functioning.[12] And so, in refusing to engage this problem proleptically, Niemeyer opens the way for enemies of the party to suggest that a communist building is obscuring or even burying its inner workings. Most of the PCF's operations take place inside a cave-like megastructure with almost no points of communication with the ground plane or the outside world. And this might give rise to doubts.

What exactly are all those Marxists doing down in those subterranean chambers? Why can't they behave like regular employees and just go up to their offices, where we could count them and know whether they were pushing paper or training with machine guns? No trusted political party needs to barricade itself inside a Platonic cave with no light or views from the outside. How could new and useful thoughts about the changing political world emerge in such a space? Such a whispering campaign might also cast a shadow of doubt over the radiant sun metaphor, and even introduce the competing figures of a black hole or troublesome boil. Indeed, a passerby could be forgiven for feeling some trepidation about this bulbous protuberance that now seems to be pressing through the earth's epidermis. As Althusser writes, 'every philosophy reproduces within itself, in one way or another, the conflict in which it finds itself compromised and caught up in the outside world'.[13]

Salle de délégation

Graffito in a University of Lyon classroom, 1968

Those inclined to pay heed to such casual slander would have seen the dome as obstinately refusing the obvious appeal of the outside – remaining in the grip of institutional bureaucracy even as tumultuous events unfolded in the real world. Many French leftists certainly felt this way about the PCF after 1968. But rather than simply accept such a critique, let us consider the protuberance from another, more enigmatic angle. Marx and Engels famously begin their *Communist Manifesto* by diagramming the haunting effect upon Europe of the 'spectre of communism': 'All the powers of old Europe have entered into a holy alliance to exorcise this spectre: Pope and Czar, Metternich and Guizot, French radicals and German police-spies.'[14] They point out its role as a powerful bogeyman, used to scare naive citizens and push politics to the right: 'Where is the party in opposition that has not been decried as communistic by its opponents in power?' Rather than allow

this power to exist only in negative form, the duo insist on owning it: 'it is high time that communists should openly, in the face of the whole world, publish their views, their aims, their tendencies and meet this nursery tale of the spectre of communism with a manifesto of the party itself'.[15] The 'manifesto', then, is the becoming concrete of what was previously only spectral, a negative threat becoming a positive position.[16] Seen in similar terms, the dome of the PCF building might concretely stage (in poured concrete) the becoming manifest of a political latency, its dramatic emergence now on the surface of the earth.

TRACKING SHOT I: FROM SAUSAGE FACTORY TO SUPERMARKET

But the dome was not completed till 1980. And back in May 1968, when Parisian students and workers rallied to take down the government, the PCF was, according to many observers associated with the New Left, strangely out of touch with the developing situation – not just the particular grievances that brought students and workers together, but also the emerging desires and new modes of thinking. As Chris Marker explains in his film *Le fond de l'air est rouge* (titled in English *A Grin Without a Cat*), the only role the theorists on place du Colonel Fabien could imagine for themselves was that of directing energies they had not initiated or anticipated. This poor performance at a key moment was, unquestionably, a concern for many thinkers on the left at the time. But French New Wave cinema – responding to the limitations of the PCF – had been developing a new set of languages for thinking politics long before 1968.

Jean-Luc Godard's *Le petit soldat*, a movie about the Algerian War, was actually made the same year as the iconic *À bout de souffle* (1960), but fell foul of the censors and was not released until 1963. Its protagonist, Bruno Forestier (Michel Subor), is an army deserter (for him, national service was not the kind of levelling experience, instilling great resourcefulness, that it appears to have been for Belmondo's character in *L'Homme de Rio*). Hoping to return to the French

ANNA KARINA
MICHEL SUBOR
a film by
JEAN-LUC
GODARD
LE
PETIT
SOLDAT
A RIALTO PICTURES RELEASE
RIALTO

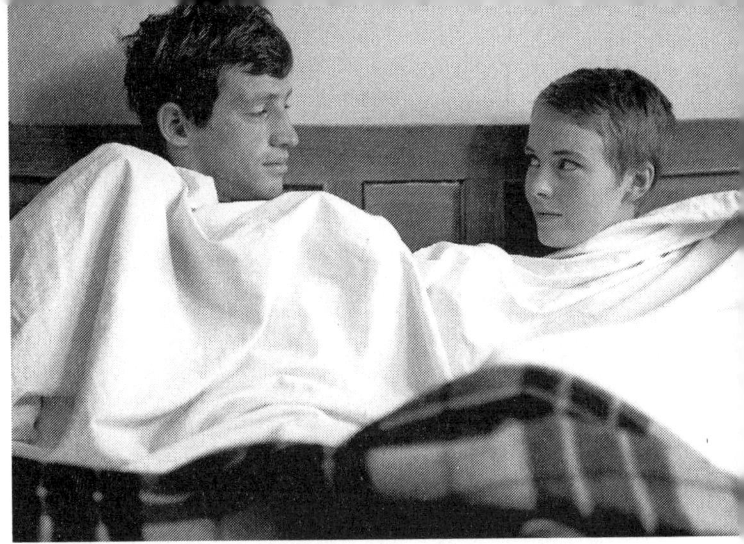

state's good graces, Forestier is vulnerable to pressure from a right-wing group who want to recruit him to assassinate supporters of Algerian independence.[1] Though he resists for most of the film, he ultimately capitulates, before seeking to escape to Brazil.

Though all of Godard's films from the mid-1960s through the mid-1970s can be seen as participating in a discussion about the philosophy of political representation, it is his *Tout va bien* (1972), a movie he co-wrote and directed with Jean-Pierre Gorin, a former student of Althusser's, that perhaps contributes most powerfully to this debate.[2] Toward the end of the film the female protagonist, Susan Dewitt (Jane Fonda), admits:

Jean-Luc Godard, Une femme est une femme, 1961 (above left); Le petit soldat, 1963 (below left); À bout de souffle, 1960 (above)

'I'm an American correspondent who doesn't correspond to anything.' The process of political re-education she has undergone since 1968 has made her feel that she no longer has a language for representing her politics – that the existing vocabulary of political representation is entirely inadequate. This is a problem the film takes

Jean-Luc Godard, Tout va bien, 1972, and stills from the tracking shot through the sausage factory (overleaf)

up programmatically in its own filmic language, and in particular through its engagement with architecture.

The two most famous scenes in *Tout va bien* are long tracking shots. The first occurs at a sausage factory, where a routine stoppage has suddenly shifted: the workers have trapped their boss in his office and taken over the company's personnel office, where they start ripping up the employment records. When Fonda's character and her husband (Yves Montand), also a reporter, arrive to cover the event, they are quickly locked in the office along with the boss (the workers intuiting that media coverage is far from neutral). Again, prevented from leaving, the boss yells: '*véritables voyous*' (real hooligans). As he does so, we get the first shot filmed with the factory's facade peeled away, the removal of the masonry allowing us to see this office in the context of the other spaces around it. We are perhaps encouraged to see this attempt to show the whole situation, to show one room's relation to another, and implicitly one 'position' in the conflict in relation to another, as an extension of the film's opening gesture: that of materialising and locating

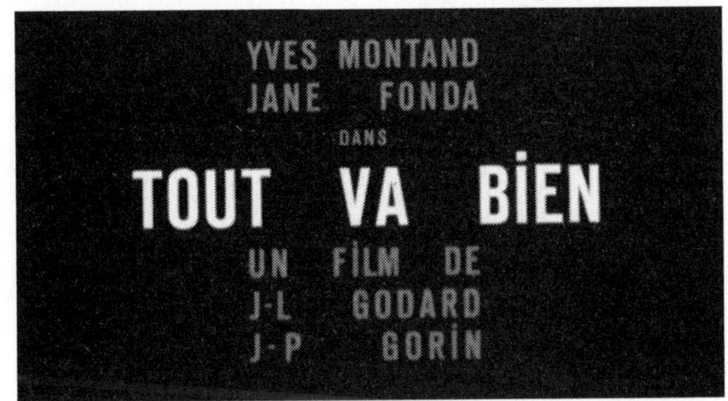

the economic reality of film. 'I want to make a film', says a male voice. 'You need money for that', responds a female voice. Immediately after this we are shown a close-up of a hand signing cheques for all aspects of the movie. This at once playful and serious attempt to materialise the constraints of filmmaking then shifts to narrative, as we learn that there will be economic pressure for the film to be a love story, and for there to be international actors.[3] Then, with these givens in place, the film tries to analyse and respond to the conditions of its birth, which essentially means having the characters begin to consider their larger social and historical situations. It is in this sense that *Tout va bien* becomes site-specific not just within the post-1968 French political landscape, but also within the media conditions that would attend any representation of that landscape, which is to say, for Godard, within the larger 'site' of filmmaking in France at that moment.

But if one imagines that the tracking shots are an attempt to reject facades in the name of penetrating, visually, into the truth, then one is left with the inaccurate idea that Godard believes that the political situation is one that can be seen through – much in the manner that pre-Althusserian Marxism proposed the opposition between ideology and class consciousness.[4] Perhaps the boss can be aligned with ideology; but neither of the two lefts that now compete with one another has a firm and final grip on something as essential as 'class consciousness'. This is one of the presumed unities that comes apart in the film. And the architectural tracking shots help Godard suggest this: they reject the discreteness of individual identities, positions or spaces, insisting instead on new ways of imagining their interrelationships. What emerges from this visual 'transparency' is anything but transparent; rather, it is a large architectural space filmed so as to reveal the social opacities that cannot simply be eradicated or explained away through the boss's discourse of efficiency or widely shared improvements in the standard of living.

In an interview in 1972 Godard compared his film with Marin Karmitz's *Coup pour coup* (*Blow for Blow*), released that year:

> *Coup pour coup* goes directly to the textile workers of Elbeuf, and makes a film with them. In my opinion he [Karmitz] skips a step. He thinks he can listen directly to what they have to say, though they've been denied a voice for so long, and that we can be of use to them with no problems. We think there is a problem which is that the very medium we use was, up until now, in the hands of those we're fighting against. Therefore, despite our good intentions, we don't completely control it.[5]

The attempt to represent workers is complicated here by the history of the media of representation – both film and TV. As Godard puts it, the expectation that workers who have never been allowed to represent themselves within these media should now be able to do so in crisp, 30-second snippets is totally ridiculous. The media's normative timing compresses 'representation' into irrelevant soundbites. Seeking to addresses these problems, Godard suggests that rather than try to work 'in the name of' a group he's not part of, he instead works from his own position. Of the tracking shots that are an invention of this position, he remarks: 'I tried to create images that were simpler and less complicated precisely to show how complex the situation is.'[6]

Godard's first tracking shot in *Tout va bien* is a short filmic essay on the problem of political representation after 1968. Fonda's character is a correspondent who doesn't correspond to anything, the film suggests, because no language comparable to the film's for showing relationships has yet entered the discourse of journalism or familiar leftist discourse, such as Marxism. This problem is underlined in the second tracking shot, which takes place in a Carrefour supermarket where, as the camera moves to the right parallel to the checkout counters, shoppers buy huge cartloads of food, clothing and alcohol. Part way through the shot we encounter a Marxist selling his book, marked down from 5.50 to 4.75 francs. Orange, not quite red, its radicality has been drained and diluted. And so, he is a fitting target for new political actors – the students – who suddenly pour into the store with their long hair, casual clothes and defiant postures. The students now test a different model of politics – one of direct action launched through the performative claim to the other shoppers: 'It's all free! Help yourselves!' Marxist bureaucracy and the rule of law are both temporarily suspended by this speech act. Now the trolleys move parallel to the picture plane, toward the exit, as we track the same space of the checkout counters for a third pass. But this time, when we get to the end, it is not freedom and successfully stolen goods that await the students, but police batons. What these new political actors encounter at the exit, then, is the old-fashioned state apparatus, without its ideological prefix.

Stills from the tracking shot through the supermarket, Tout va bien, 1972

carrefo

Like Godard's first tracking shot in *Tout va bien*, this one also uses architecture to develop a more complex language of spatial and political analysis – in a way that might allow the Susan Dewitts of the world to feel that they could once again become correspondents who *do* correspond to something. In both cases, there is a new vocabulary of desire: for the hostage-takers it's a language of pleasure that rejects a certain kind of socialist realist version of their daily lives; for the Carrefour thieves (until the state's policing power intervenes), it's a Dionysian excess that dispenses with the abstract, future-oriented discourse of the Marxists. The first shot has richer suggestions for how we might think about architecture, but they both point to dilemmas that emerge when an overly clear Old Left confronts a still inchoate New Left of emergent desires. Through these two tracking shots, Godard points to the limits of existing political vocabularies in a way that is ultimately more concrete and evocative than just about any 'theory' from this period.

That is, the filmmaker points to the basic dilemma that confronts Niemeyer's building: the desire for an extreme leftism that doesn't look and feel like familiar Communist Party politics. And politics that, especially after 1968, could be satirised in ways Godard does in *Tout va bien* by having the bumbling party rep standing in a vast supermarket landscape hawking a merely orange little red book. Could a building make Marxism red again, while healing the split between the emergent desires of the students and the ossified politics of the party bureaucrats? To do so, it would need to entertain the legitimacy of these new desires, and the importance of these new actors, more seriously than Marxism had done up to then.

TRACKING SHOT II: FROM GIBBET TO UNION

When Niemeyer offered to design the building on place du Colonel Fabien for free, he was taking on not only the massive problem of representing the Communist Party, but also the dilemma of an extremely loaded site in Paris's nineteenth arrondissement with a complicated and perhaps contradictory history. The roughly triangular, 5,000m^2 sloping patch of ground between avenue Mathurin Moreau and boulevard de la Villette had previously been the site of a trade union and a university for workers.[1] But its real trauma and glory came earlier. From the thirteenth to the seventeenth century, a building just up the hill from place du Colonel Fabien had served the kings of France as their main execution stage. There, the bodies of enemies of the state (criminals or traitors) were hung and displayed on a terrifyingly vast superstructure, the Gibbet of Montfaucon.[2] In Viollet-le-Duc's drawing from 1856, it's pictured as a three-storey masonry structure resting on a large rusticated base. Imagine Giuseppe Terragni's Casa del Fascio in Como tipped on its side, and you have some idea of this disturbingly 'rational' pre-modern death rectangle. Niemeyer's site for the PCF headquarters was linked, then, from its early history, with the most extreme forms of state spectacle and power, what Althusser refers to as the repressive state apparatus, though the gallows appears not to have been used after 1626, and it was dismantled in 1760.

Viollet-le-Duc, Gibbet of Montfaucon, Paris, 1856

Giuseppe Terragni, Casa del Fascio, Como, 1936

Then, in the 1780s, the site became one of the new city barriers, part of the *mur des Fermiers généraux*, overseen by Antoine Lavoisier and designed by Claude-Nicolas Ledoux. Though the best surviving image – a watercolour sketch – makes the building seem like a calm pastoral edge to the capital, in fact these neoclassical structures (the most famous of which are the surviving Rotonde de la Villette and the Barrière d'Enfer) were designed not to protect the city, but to extract taxes on goods entering Paris. As Anthony Vidler has explained:

> None of Ledoux's designs, projected or built, were so immediately and consistently the objects of outrage, criticism and condemnation as were the approximately 60 tollgates or *barrières* of Paris. Erected in the last years of the *ancien régime* in secrecy and haste, they were inevitably seen as the visible emblems of fiscal tyranny, enforced by the hated *Ferme Générale*. Their monumentality and strange forms, exaggerated traditional architectural motifs in scale and placement to the point of caricature, seemed to confirm the economic profligacy of the regime.[3]

A French pun from the period, playing on the shared syllable (*mur*) in the words for 'wall' and 'murmuring', locates the wall as a source of rumbling discontent: *Le mur murant Paris rend Paris murmurant* ('The wall walling Paris keeps Paris murmuring'). The writer Louis-Sébastien Mercier describes how a sadistic bureaucratic process turned ordinary, law-abiding citizens into criminals. 'Everyday persons of the most unquestioned probity may be heard lying like lawyers at the barriers. Morality never disapproves a lie told to the customs.'[4] Separate stamps of approval had to be obtained for every single item an individual wanted to bring in: 'Payment involves a visit to ten offices, and the procuring of 20 signatures for each solitary bale or bag. If your luggage includes a book or two, that means another little journey to the rue du Foin, where yet another inspector approves or condemns your taste in literature.'[5]

These everyday associations with crushing bureaucracy and a larger tradition of tyranny did not stop Ledoux from investing the tollgates with a 'didactic role', as Vidler notes. Conceived as 'paradigms of combination and characterisation' of classical styles – each slightly different from the next – the gates were intended to provide 'object lessons for architect and

Animal fights at the Barrière du Combat, Paris

Barrière des Fourneaux and Barrière du Combat, Paris, 1819

citizen' alike.[6] For Ledoux, they operated as emblems of 'public virtues assembled in a circle to level the public mind ... constructions whose diversity slakes the thirst of desire'.[7] Take away those mobilising intentions, and what's left is a pedagogical architecture without an institutional undergirding – a conceptual ruin, even when the building has physically survived, as all but four of the 62 gatehouses have done.

The gate at what's now place du Colonel Fabien was initially called the Barrière St Louis, but it soon became known as the Barrière du Combat, after the nearby blood sports arena. Here, on Sundays and Mondays, packs of domestic dogs would be pitted against wild boars, wolves, bears and bulls, while Parisians screamed and jostled one another and, of course, bet on the outcomes. The larger wild animals, which also included

Konstantin Melnikov, Soviet pavilion, Paris, 1925

panthers and leopards, tended to be muzzled and even bled in advance to even up the odds. The fact that the institution had been relocated outside the city walls (it had previously been on rue de Sèvres, where Le Corbusier would one day have his office) gives a sense of the growing unease about this particular form of leisure. In fact, this gruesome spectacle didn't go on for much longer: by 1830 its popularity had waned and it seems finally to have come to an end around 1845–50.

Soon after this, the site of the arena began to be used as a dump. How long it operated in this capacity is not clear, but we do know that it had been cleaned up by the 1920s, as the Soviet pavilion was moved there at the end of the 1925 International Exhibition of Decorative and Industrial Arts. Designed by Konstantin Melnikov, this was a constructivist building, expressing the early, experimental phase of Soviet architecture before the tamped-down repressions of social realism.[8] It took the form of a rectangle that had been split diagonally, with a staircase along this seam, and a kind of exploded roof above, consisting of tilted panels rotated up from the roof line about 30 degrees and placed on alternate sides of the rift, so that they crossed in the middle and let light and air into the stair. The walls were almost entirely square glass panels, and along the side of the stair was a triangular constructivist tower composed of unenclosed vertical elements and diagonal cross-braces. Certainly, this was the most dynamic, most experimental, architecture in the exhibition. The buildings on the site, then, allow us to trace a history of state power and spectacle, from the Gibbet – a display of the dire consequences of betraying the nation – to the

Soviet pavilion, a perhaps surprising advertisement for a cosmopolitan internationalism. In providing a permanent location for an exhibition pavilion designed as a proselytising example of anti-capitalist construction – a built fragment of the new Soviet social and spatial order – the state was showing an open-handedness, an apparent lack of fear toward a potential enemy, that was perhaps designed to inoculate Parisians against the threat. Still, in a pre-Stalin moment of optimism, Melnikov's pavilion must have been a powerful project.

The symbolism of the pavilion was not lost on the Nazi forces occupying Paris. In 1942, it was bulldozed into oblivion.[9] And yet, the Nazis were not alone in rejecting the modernism of the pre-war years: the PCF did so as well, in line with the Soviet state. A socialist–realist aesthetic was the official Soviet style well into the 1950s, and returns to any kind of modernism were only very gradual. So whatever one makes of the PCF's choice of an architect aligned with Le Corbusier (who, again, the left loved to hate), it is also worth emphasising

Le Corbusier and Pierre Jeanneret, Pavillion de l'Esprit Nouveau, Paris, 1925

Pierre George, aka Colonel Fabien, 1939

4.12.1939
779038

that a modernist building had only been a viable option for a very brief period at the time of the commission.

Of course, the one other structure at the 1925 exhibition that could hold a candle to Melnikov's was the Esprit Nouveau pavilion designed by Le Corbusier and Pierre Jeanneret.[10] Alongside machine-made furniture and a carefully selected collection of cubist and purist paintings, the pavilion displayed a model of the Plan Voisin. The second major urban commission in Le Corbusier's career, after the 1922 Ville Contemporaine, it envisioned housing three million people in a series of 60-storey apartment buildings.[11] Even more controversially, it proposed to do this by redeveloping Paris, levelling hundreds of blocks in the existing city. Whether the plan was conceived as workable or imagined more as a provocation remains open to question.[12] But the very fact that the plan *was* debated helped to launch Le Corbusier's career, or rather, to shift it from paper to physical architecture, since many commissions for houses in and around Paris emerged during the 1925 fair.

Another connection Le Corbusier made at the exhibition was none other than Melnikov himself, whose pavilion he admired, considering it the only other truly modern building there. Melnikov, in turn, invited the Swiss architect to travel to the Soviet Union. When Le Corbusier arrived, he was delighted to discover that his polemical writings had been translated into Russian.[13] In Moscow, Le Corbusier not only delivered lectures and gave interviews, he also designed the Tsentrosoyuz building for the Central Union of Consumer Cooperatives, which might be considered an important precedent for Niemeyer's PCF headquarters. Le Corbusier's project also used curtain-walls to organise the offices, and counterposed these with a sculptural object that would house the assembly hall. However, it did not sink any significant portion of its programme underground, perhaps because the site was slightly more generous. But while the Tsentrosoyuz building was fairly widely published, it was Le Corbusier's unrealised proposal for the Palace of the Soviets (1932) that was more famous – and famously rejected by Stalin in favour of a neo-classical wedding-cake deemed an acceptable socialist–realist building, a reminder of what official Soviet aesthetics had become by the 1930s. Niemeyer would certainly have been aware of both of Le Corbusier's Soviet projects, and of the specific history of the working-class Belleville neighbourhood where he found his site.

'Colonel Fabien' was in fact the codename of a PCF member – a hero of the resistance, Pierre George, who in 1941 had shot and killed a German soldier in revenge for the execution of Samuel Tyszelman for taking part in a demonstration against the occupation. This initial act of resistance set in motion a series of assassinations and reprisals that would ultimately claim the lives of some 500 French hostages over the following months. Though 'Fabien' was arrested and tortured in 1943, he managed to escape and was ultimately dispatched not by the Germans but by a landmine. The decision to rename place du Combat in his honour, then, was an equivocal gesture: while invoking the possibility of resistance in the face of terrifying power, it also pointed to the Germans' systematic exercise of that power on an exponentially greater scale, and thus to the site's older role as symbolic killing field for the state.

Travelling northwest along Metro line 2, the next stop after Colonel Fabien is Jaurès, named after the early twentieth-century socialist, Jean Jaurès, who was assassinated on the eve of the First World War in part because of his anti-militarism. Political traffic, too, has increasingly gone in this direction, away from the PCF toward the socialists, toward Mitterrand, who became president in 1981, the year after the PCF headquarters were completed, and, more recently, toward Jean-Luc Mélenchon, leader of the largest left-wing group in the National Assembly. But let us imagine a pedestrian heading in the opposite direction, from Jaurès, along the double-lane boulevard de la Villette, toward place du Colonel Fabien, where eight different streets feed into the elliptical space. On stepping into the square, one might miss the protruding dome amid the buses, plane trees and perennial construction sheds. But for the more attentive, the PCF's bulging assembly hall is identifiable at almost any point along the route from Jaurès – first, perhaps, through foreshortening, as a kind of expansion of the curving profile of a moving car or truck. Then, when one arrives at the south side of the square, the hall peeks out a bit more, though as yet discreetly. Still only partially visible behind tree trunks, news kiosks, temporary traffic barriers, port-a-johns and buses, the white dome is now less of a possible mirage than a mysterious presence. We can see that it sits on a concrete base that tilts down toward the square, an inviting triangular entry plane to a garden. As we approach from the south, the dome rises, gradually separating itself from street signage, green baskets of docked bikes and a bulbous Guimard metro entrance. But when we cross boulevard de la Villette and begin to take in the PCF from its own block, we become aware of a large metal fence that prevents us from coming closer. From here, it is also clear that this mysterious white protrusion that has captured our attention depends, for its role as a three-dimensional actor, on being framed against the backdrop of a curtain-wall, its obvious stage. Nor is this set always a secondary element. In the spring of 2022, the top two floors became a massive billboard: a photographic portrait of the party's candidate for the French presidential election next to two columns of text – above in white letters, 'Le 10 avril', and below, in huge yellow letters, 'VOTONS Fabien

Jean Jaurés addresses the crowd at Le Pré-Saint-Gervais, Paris, 1913; the PCF building promoting Communist Party presidential candidate Fabien Roussel, 2022 (overleaf)

FABIEN
ROUSSEL
Fabien ROUS
La France de

ours heureux

ROUSSEL'. All this against a salmon pink background. The PCF's curving glass facade had become a hand-made, analogue version of an LED screen, 'speaking' to its urban surroundings in clearer and firmer tones than the 'endearingly gentle' dome.[1]

And still, the city and the country at large failed to heed the message. Roussel rallied just 2.3 percent of the vote in the first round, a poor showing compared to Mélenchon, who got 22 percent, trailing only slightly behind Marine Le Pen's 23 percent. Had the two leftist parties come together, they could have shut out Le Pen and fielded their own candidate against Emmanuel Macron in the second round. The PCF, however, continues to resist this coming together, partly as payback for the Mitterrand years, but also, evidently, as a matter of self-preservation.

When the PCF headquarters was completed in the 1980s, most leftists still believed that powerful international organisations (both economic and political – from Nato and the EU to the United Nations) offered the best hope of advancing society. Many would rethink their position as the economic disparities of globalisation became increasingly apparent, but this earlier moment of almost utopian internationalism coincided with Niemeyer's central involvement in designing what would become some of the central institutions of neo-liberalism. Niemeyer, like many others, initially saw globalisation as a positive development. His aspiration in designing both the UN building and Brasília was for a 'world without borders; an open world ... [but] today this world believes in neo-liberalism'; here, greater access to consumer goods was equated with personal happiness. Later in life, he recommended that 'before becoming enthusiastic about globalisation, you should first of all look at the damage this invention is doing in Africa'. As for the rest of the world, he noted 'North American imperialism pursues a single aim: to incorporate our economy and our firms. Latin America needs to demonstrate solidarity and fight against America. I am not talking about making war, we have no objection to the Americans, only to their politics.'[2]

As winner of the competition for the United Nations complex in Manhattan, Niemeyer was largely responsible for designing the most important architectural manifestation of postwar humanitarianism – a role that offers another line of access to the complicated question of how one might frame the politics of his buildings. Niemeyer was asked to sit on a board of architectural consultants, overseen by Wallace Harrison, who would both submit and select a design. But Le Corbusier had different ideas: he thought that Niemeyer should not submit a project, but should instead support his own proposal, which located both the UN assembly hall and the council chambers in a building near the centre of the site, and had the secretariat tower at the south end. Niemeyer initially agreed, but after urging from Harrison and Max Abramovitz he eventually submitted a project – and it was selected; or rather, it was decided that the Niemeyer plan would serve as the main concept, but that some of Le Corbusier's ideas would also inform the design. Le Corbusier again pressured Niemeyer to shift his plans, which he did to a large degree, though not as much as the Swiss-French visionary would have liked. Of this tense interaction, Niemeyer remarks:

Oscar Niemeyer, working on the design for the UN headquarters in his studio in the RKO building, New York, 1947 (and overleaf)

> It would be natural, in light of the episode I have described, for me to speak of Le Corbusier in a less friendly manner. But this is not the case. I remember him today with the same enthusiasm I felt the first time we met, 40 years ago, when we went to pick him up at the airport. He seemed to be an architect-genius come down from heaven. If, on the one hand, he was sometimes overly eager to make his own architecture, on the other hand I always felt he was a human being who carried a message, a paean to beauty that could not be silenced. Accept and understand him: that is what I always tried to do.[3]

Other leftists might well have disputed the suggestion that Le Corbusier was heaven-sent. After offering his services to the Soviet state, he had displayed considerable political flexibility, working for Vichy and writing to Mussolini outlining his vision for a new capital in Addis Ababa after Italy's invasion of Ethiopia – though somehow this doesn't seem to have troubled the committee that selected the architectural luminaries for the UN competition. The resulting UN building is a compromise that does not rank among either Le Corbusier's or Niemeyer's best schemes. But regardless of how one understands the power struggles between the two architects, the discourse of the United Nations operates in an interesting tension with the Marxism and post-colonialism with which Niemeyer is often otherwise associated. To over-simplify, the United Nations is a project about universal humanism, whereas Niemeyer's other clients and sites were, in various ways, necessarily

23
23

engaged in a critique of humanism in the name of historical materialism. Certainly, Niemeyer himself often sounded classically humanist – speaking, for instance, of his attraction to women's bodies as the source for his vocabulary of curves. Nor is he often quoted as participating in the historical critique of humanism. Yet his life-long commitment to communism and post-colonialism would likely have made him aware of at least some aspect of this critique.[4] When it comes to positioning architecture in relation to politics, he leans toward the idea that architecture merely reflects, rather than instigates, social transformation. In this respect, he distances himself from Le Corbusier, who according to Niemeyer, 'thought that architecture can change life... I don't agree at all with that view. I believe exactly the opposite is true. It is life that influences architecture.'[5]

Sketch of the preliminary design for the UN headquarters by Hugh Ferriss, 1947

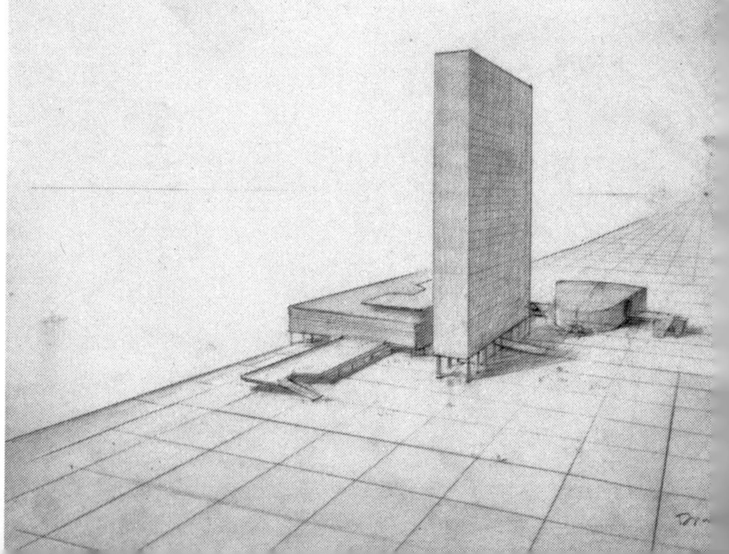

Oscar Niemeyer on the site of an office block in Rio de Janeiro, 1950, photo Kurt Hutton

But perhaps the question here is the threshold at which we acknowledge an influence. If revolution is that threshold, then yes, life influences architecture. But if our marker is more subtle, then surely architecture does change the humans who use it. In fact, Niemeyer's statement might paradoxically be seen as an attempt to align his buildings with party discourse, rather than to account for the ambitions that seem latent within them. But if his explicit political stance was somewhere between the official PCF position and the more ambitious Sartrean commitment, then he might at least have been curious about the emergence of Althusserian structuralist Marxism. Sartre himself certainly was, and in a 1969 interview he defended Althusser from the charge that the latter's work was scholastic and not connected to praxis.

Althusser's critique of humanism essentially took aim at the idea of consciousness, which he perceived as inward and subjective, and thus abandoned, turning instead to the external domain of 'structure'. A corollary of this position was the rejection of what, from Marx to Lukács, had been the founding opposition between a mystified group of bourgeois subjects – dupes to a 'false consciousness' or ideology – and the proletariat, who can attain class consciousness and thus represent the forces of history and truth.[6] In shifting from consciousness to structure, Althusser wanted the latter term to take on a disruptive, materialist resonance – similar to how Marx had upended Hegelian talk of spirit and ideas with his emphasis on objective, physical reality.[7] Althusser argued that ideology was not a mere illusion: it could not be simply stripped away to recover the truth. Always operating at some distance from truth, ideology constitutes positions, and indeed individuals as subjects. If it is a 'system of representations', 'in the majority of cases these representations have nothing to do with "consciousness" ... it is above all *structures* that they impose on the vast majority of men'.[8]

Even though it might seem reasonable to object that subjects internalise these structures via consciousness, Althusser was adamant in turning against the term, which he associated with inwardness. By contrast, 'structure' seemed to work because it came at us with force from the exterior world of things. Structures demanded, compelled; we confronted or banged into them. They could physically control crowds or offer shelter. They had the substantial reality of the city's most solid buildings.

Could one of these buildings, designed by a Marxist architect at this very moment, help us to focus such a new understanding of 'structure'? Could a building even dramatise its own status as an embodiment of ideology? Up until then, ideology had been central in the struggle for authentic self-representation and self-knowledge: it was the false consciousness one needed to throw off before one could find the reliable, materialist knowledge of class consciousness. But in locating the persistence of ideology even here – even in the way that a party must represent itself to itself – Althusser introduced a set of new problems for Marxist representations and representations of Marxism alike: 'In ideology, men do indeed express, not the relation between them and their conditions of existence, but *the way* they live [this] relation.'[9] Because ideology involves an imaginary relationship to the real, it opens up a gap in representation. While we cannot simply close this gap, we can mobilise it.

But what might such a mobilisation look like? Rejecting the belief that there is something realistic about socialist realism and something purely functional about functionalism might be a good place to start.[10] Not much of a critical outlook is required to dismantle the former misconception, but the hold of functionalism has proved harder to shake – even if it seems obvious today that the buildings of Le Corbusier, for instance, embodied an elaborate fantasy of modern life, rather than a simple solution to purely functional requirements. Niemeyer's own rejection of the rhetoric of functionalism

Oscar Niemeyer, conceptual sketches, 1967 (overleaf)

allowed him to articulate what would become, as Styliane Philippou has noted, 'a visual mythology for Brazil' – a founding fiction of a world without right angles.[11] 'I made use of the limitless resources of reinforced concrete to enter a universe of curves, truncated planes, oblique facades, and diverse supports ... a world of strange, unforeseen forms, of which all the essentials are now part of the vocabulary of Brazilian architecture.'[12]

Niemeyer's turn to the concrete curve can be seen not just as the emergence of a new, more corporeal architectural language, but as an attempt to construe the orthogonal as a form of repression. For the mythological

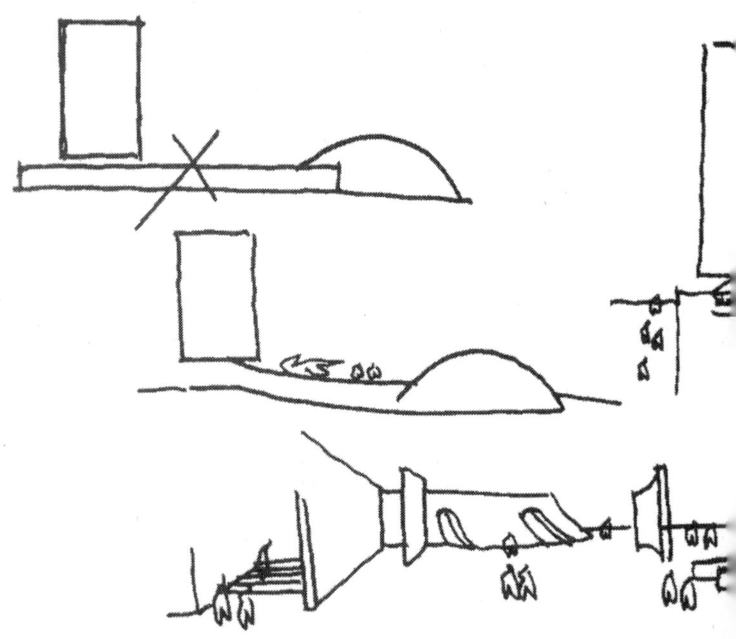

space of his architecture to open up most enticingly, and for its ideological dimensions to take hold, Niemeyer had to present an architecture of right angles as a sort of preliminary phase: one whose needless conventionalism and inattentiveness to the demands of the body would be transcended by his own new way of building.

To maintain the power and consistency of this mythology – a project in itself – Niemeyer often relied on a strategy of showing scenarios that he had first considered only to then reject. Early representations of the PCF building, for example, include several sketches that show the possibility of either an orthogonal plinth

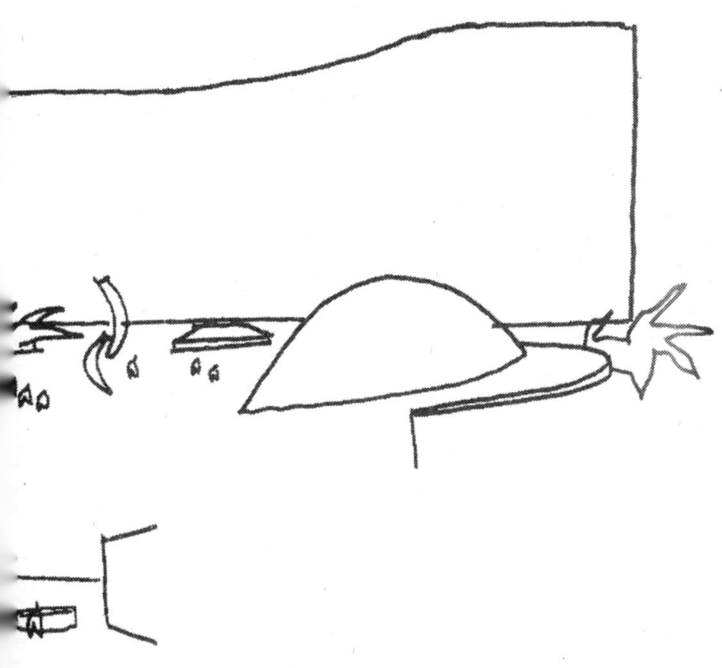

with the slab rising above it or a discrete building on taller pilotis sitting on a flat ground plane. Within the same set of sketches, these options are then crossed out and replaced with the sloping ground he in fact developed. It remains unclear whether these drawings reflect the actual, real-time emergence of the concept of an organic ground plane, or are instead theatrical flourishes designed to reassure the viewer that he had in fact considered other options.[13] Nor can we establish with certainty that the primary valence of this gesture is the rejection of normative office culture, rather than the need to protect the party (with a material more solid than glass) from the repercussions of communist outrages in places like Hungary. What seems clearer is that, however the concept emerged, Niemeyer felt its alternatives should be retained, if only to show that they had been considered and negated. More precisely, the older fantasies of a normative modernism had to be shown as inadequate before the breakthrough of the curving ground plane of the building's cosmology was introduced.

Given this, maybe the curving solar system of Niemeyer's building could be seen as a version of ideology that knows itself as such: the plan-based reconciliation of the hammer and sickle; the turn away from the familiar and placeless office interior toward a thin building in which workers control their environment through operable windows; the sinuously moulded ground plane that brings the acolyte on a curving path through a garden and up to a cave-like entrance, passing by the magical dome along the way, which we can now see compels its surroundings into its orbit, literally bending the elegant curtain-wall of offices.

Next to one of the sketches of the sloping ground plane is another depicting tiny figures wandering from the street to the front esplanade, which is shown as a kind of sculpture garden in which the dome, the paired curves of the abstract sculpture and the cantilevered plane of the basement entrance offer focal points for the people freely exploring the site. Sadly, the explosion of violence in late 1960s politics – and in particular the response to Soviet repression in Eastern Europe – persuaded the PCF that it was necessary to have a metal fence run around the whole perimeter of their property, making the park enclosed, private. After 1968, the people apparently needed to be protected from the people.

The PCF's curtain-wall, designed by Jean Prouvé, operates as a stage-set or backdrop for the building's dome. But the structural organisation of the glass facade demands attention in itself, with its changing interrelations of opacity, reflection and transparency often shifting into enticing ambiguity, especially at dusk. Above the concrete base, each of the building's six floors is marked by a dark horizontal band. At the top, the facade is completed by a small extra section, perhaps one third of a bay or floor. Vertically, each office is marked by three glass bays framed by four lighter metal mullions. In the middle of each of these units is an operable square panel. The effect of this is to introduce a grid within a grid, made up of a series of ideal forms within the shifting vertical surface of glass. If the lighting conditions are right, one can stand at the fence at the edge of the site and catch the sky poking through the building's roof onto its top floors. Below this, the bays now take on a slightly pale grey cast, seeming to reflect the sky, while an expressive profile made up of the reflections of the neighbouring buildings across the square emerges at the bottom of the facade. But as we look toward the southern end of the building, the curve of the facade gradually dissipates this effect, giving way to a more consistent dark blue opacity, a view of glass and steel *as* glass and steel. Individual rooms show up volumetrically on the facade depending on whether their lights are on. At times, especially from closer up, it's possible to see the white linear forms of hanging fluorescent lights, sharp lines receding in perspective, as well as curtains, muted white rectangles that punctuate the dark blue. At some points during the day, the rectangles of the operable windows almost disappear, while the curtains behind them now catch the light. At other times, any sense of interiority vanishes and the facade becomes a cool, solid surface of dark blue that only reflects clouds, sky and the surrounding architecture.

Regardless of how much Niemeyer knew or cared about it when he designed this structure, structuralism was undeniably a central challenge to the place of Marxism in the landscape of French social and intellectual life at the time of the commission. And this fact pre-empts a shift in our investigation: an acknowledgement that as important as Althusser's contact with the movement may have been, it was in many ways an exception. Most Marxists perceived structuralism as an apolitical turn away from the diachronic forces of history to the synchronic stasis of system.[1] While syntheses between structuralism and Marxism certainly occurred, and characterised some of the most innovative thinking in France at the time, from Lévi-Strauss to Althusser to Barthes, structuralism could only emerge after 1956, when orthodox Marxism began to lose its hold on left-leaning intellectuals. It filled the vacuum left by inadequate explanations of the events in Hungary and increasing knowledge of the actual workings of Stalinism. Structuralism, then, emerged as competition to Marxism, not as a complement.[2]

Marxism's immediate critiques of structuralism stressed its apolitical turn. But more recently

structuralism has been seen as a key agent in 'the ideological struggles' by which the French socialists gradually triumphed 'over their communist adversaries in their dispute over leadership of the French left'.[3] Using Jacques Attali's influential *Noise: The Political Economy of Music* (1977) to focus this transformation, historian of music Eric Drott argues that Cold War funders were drawn to figures like Claude Lévi-Strauss and Roman Jakobson because the cybernetics and information theory they promoted seemed to offer 'a more rational and less conflictual postwar order'.[4]

Drott proposes that 'the valorisation of information as a force for social progress' was a response 'to transformations then taking place in the French economy', in particular the expansion of the new middle classes, those 'engaged in intellectual as opposed to manual labour'.[5] For this emergent social group, Attali's 'valorisation of information' seems to offer a 'strategic ... trade-off': sacrificing some 'social protections' they are offered 'greater self-determination' in 'a marked contrast with the statism of the Parti *communiste*'. This stance is what Drott calls an artistic critique of capitalism: 'It was capitalism's inability to satisfy individual aspirations, not its unjust redistribution of social wealth from one class to another, that came to be regarded as its principal failing'.[6] Such artistic critique, which for Drott would include all the non-classically Marxist theory and film I've examined, merely smooths rather than contests the operations of capitalism and thus co-opts 'the liberatory impulses unleashed after 1968' in service of a 'post-Fordist regime of accumulation'. Whatever one makes of the affinities between Attali's work and a nascent neo-liberalism of the left and left centre, it is nonetheless the case that, by the mid-1970s, Marxism in France had failed. To dismiss all attempts to articulate new modes of desire, Deleuze and Guattari as much as Attali, as mere 'artistic critiques of capitalism' that leave the real questions (of social relations) unanswered is thus, I think, to appeal to the traditional Marxist terms and authority in a world that has just demonstrated their inadequacy.

Niemeyer's commission, then, might well be framed as a response to this waning of Marxist power and prestige and the party's concomitant desire to appear 'open'

(building in a way that embraced modernism, in the process developing affinities with emergent revolutions across the globe – particularly in Latin America – and with the most contemporary elements of Parisian intellectual life).[7] But an official stance of openness did not of course mean that the PCF actually recognised all of

Gilles Deleuze and Félix Guattari, Paris, 1980

its potential allies and was willing to embrace not just the structuralism that Lévi-Strauss had popularised, but also the post-structuralism that was, by 1967, beginning to operate as its successor. And so if Althusser points to the limitations of a base–superstructure model of culture, and also suggests that ideology is never merely the opposite of truth or class consciousness, and if Godard has his New Left political activists in *Tout va bien* pointing to a larger world of experiences that can't quite come into focus through the Marxist analysis of everyday life, Deleuze and Guattari's *Anti-Oedipus* comes closest of all to focalizing these new questions and demands. In it, desire is neither associated with lack nor contained within the Oedipal family, but instead set loose within a network of temporary energy sources or assemblages, which open the subject to the world.

But how might Niemeyer's language at the PCF headquarters have looked to a new generation who sympathised with this post-structural expansion of terms? Even if the events of 1968 happened a year after it went into construction, the building was still being designed during a moment when many of the older certainties about Marxism were crumbling. Framing a link between the expanded language of desire in the PCF headquarters and *Anti-Oedipus* would no doubt require more than projecting the division between paranoia and schizophrenia onto Niemeyer's contrast between the enclosed, inward-looking dome space and the porous curtain-wall. Moreover, such a schematic analogy might leave us admiring the seeming transparency of the building and bemoaning its mysterious caves; and yet it is the fantasies generated by the central cave and its surrounding caverns that actually put the work more closely, if paradoxically, into sympathy with Deleuze and Guattari.

Rather than a theatre of representation, a realistic modelling of the outside world, the cave is a space of mysterious desire and compelling repetition, and perhaps – through the otherworldly effect of its white ceiling elements, stage proscenium and red-leather seating rows – a spaceship-like machine whose passengers might experience the dissolution of their discrete egos and hierarchised organs into new modes of conjunction both with one another and with the strange surfaces and lights of the building itself. 'In the theatre of repetition', Deleuze writes, 'we experience pure forces, dynamic lines in space which act without intermediary upon the spirit, and link it directly with nature and history.'[8]

While Deleuze's later exploration of the baroque fold has obvious parallels with Niemeyer's practice, his earlier work and his collaborations with Félix Guattari perhaps speak more directly to the philosophical and social crises of the late 1960s. Indeed, Niemeyer's rejection of functionalism in favour of eros and fantasy parallels the philosophers' attempt to liberate the constricted world of Oedipus:

> By placing the distorting mirror of incest before desire (that's what you wanted, isn't it?), desire is shamed, stupefied, it is placed in a situation without exit, it is easily persuaded to deny 'itself' in the name of the more important interests of civilisation (what if everyone did the same, what if everyone married his mother or kept his sister for himself? There would no longer be any differentiation, any exchanges possible). We must act quickly and soon.[9]

Nor is their critique limited to psychoanalysis. Against the Marxist relegation of desire to secondary status, they counter: 'It is not possible to attribute a special form of existence to desire, a mental or psychic reality that is presumably different from the material

LE FOND
DE L'AIR
EST ROUGE

Montage et bande sonore
CHRIS.MARKER
Producteur délégué ISKRA
Distribution Pari Films

reality of social production' (30). While this was one of the richest critiques of Marxism coming out of 1968, Chris Marker's usefully complements it. The English title of his elegiac film essay on the failure of 1968, *A Grin Without a Cat* (1976), comes from the idea of an advance guard of guerrillas (like the initial forces of Castro, and the later ones of Che) who improvise in real time, rather than represent official party policy. The movie suggests that the historical window for actions of this kind will soon be closed: in a terrifying interview with Marker, an American military expert suggests that the lessons the US has learned from such movements (especially the Cuban Revolution) will make such coups almost impossible in the future. And as much as it is in the interest of the US to broadcast such claims, the movie also seems to believe them. Unlike Godard's films from the period, this is not a work devoted to developing a new filmic language for understanding emergent divisions on the left or problems underlying political action. Though certainly innovative in how it mobilises found footage, sound and voice-over, this is a film that reflects on failure without proposing a new intervention designed to solve it. Still, the fundamental conceit of a grin without a cat helps us think about what went wrong for Marxists in 1968, when an advance guard of students and workers lost contact with the PCF, which had long imagined itself as being the base for revolution. Why groups of leftists began to act on their own, independent of party planning, and

Chris Marker, Le fond de l'air est rouge, 1976 (and overleaf)

why the party wasn't quick enough to support them, was precisely what the PCF was now called upon to explain and remedy, neither of which it could quite do. In focusing on this inexplicable gap, Marker is of course not lamenting a failure of discipline, but rather philosophising about the nature of this non-functional relay between political levels: the space between the grin and the cat, between the expression and the base, between the articulation and the planning centre, between a curtain-wall facade and the cave beneath it.

POST-CORBUSIAN BAROQUE

Like many of Niemeyer's buildings, the PCF headquarters wears its conspicuous engineering on its sleeve, or at least on its facade and pilotis. Though from the distance of the street these elements may seem entirely Corbusian, up close certain mysteries emerge. The very fact that some of the building's windows open, for instance, might be considered post-Corbusian, in that they allow the Communist Party office workers a degree of agency that the older architect was famous, at times, for refusing. The Swiss master had seen internal air-conditioning (not supplemented by operable windows) as allowing autonomy from the climatic demands of the site. The independent air-conditioned temperature he sought was, for him, a building's 'exact breathing'.[1] In fact, Niemeyer and Prouvé first designed the PCF building's facade in a Corbusian manner – that is, without operable windows. But Prouvé modified his design after the communists objected, not so much on ecological as on ideological grounds: American buildings depended on air-conditioning, and opposition to that outlook was fundamental. The PCF was given an air-conditioning system, but it was hidden under all the sculpted blocks on the roof and used only as needed, and not continually.[2] Party members could thus feel superior to the Americans so long as they looked straight ahead, focusing on the operable windows in their facade, rather than letting their attention drift up to the HVAC system on the roof or down to their private cars in the basement parking lot.

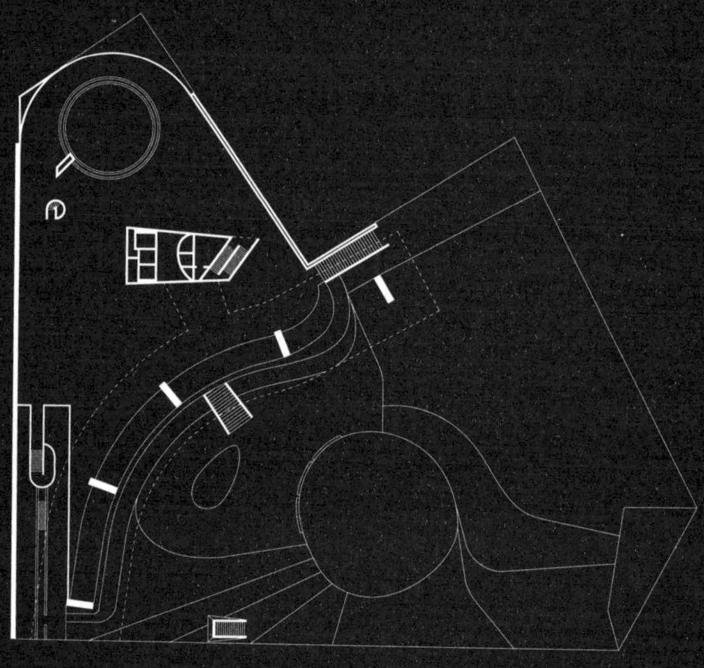

Ground-floor plan

Moving from the curtain-wall to the interior, we can see that the PCF headquarters also has, at least in its upper floors, a free plan – that is, a plan in which the division of spaces is not coincident with the expression of structure. Access to these floors is provided by a large circulation element, combining elevators and a staircase. Together with a smaller emergency stair, also in poured concrete and closer to rue Mathurin Moreau, these two circulation towers hang off the back of the office bar as sculptural elements visible only from the PCF's rear courtyard. In entering this space, we are perhaps surprised by the size of the larger of these elements, which is a kind of crushed rectangle connected to the building's main spine by a trapezoidal hallway, the one component of the PCF headquarters that might be described as brutalist. The concrete tower is punctured by rectangular windows below, and by air vents and a horizontal window above. But perhaps the most surprising element of this courtyard is a circular opening (made of poured concrete and glass) that brings light and air one storey down into the basement. Open as it is, this sunken courtyard operates as an inversion of the dome that the building presents to the public in the front courtyard. Here, in the most private and protected corner of the site, where the curtain-wall's less elegant verso is broken up by these prominent circulation pieces, Niemeyer allows light, air and views to descend into the basement through this large perforation of the ground plane. In the process, the programmatic sealing and separating that governs the frontal dome gives way to an open and airy subterranean garden.

Having visited this one spot from which it is possible to take in the full mass and extent of the PCF headquarters' mostly hidden stairs and elevators, let us now use them to go up to the top of the building, where we arrive at the roof terrace – or perhaps we might call it the HVAC garden, with its stepped concrete benches that cover the air-conditioning units. Writing in *The Architectural Review*, Sherban Cantacuzino presents the problem of resolving this infrastructural garden as the second of two 'anxious moments during construction':

> The planning of the upper floors – the dining rooms on the sixth floor open out on to terraces which lead to the roof garden above – reminds one that the building is a progeny of a Corbusian prototype in which the modelling of the roof surface, like that of the facades, was to be explored in three dimensions as an act of liberation. But Niemeyer had to accept the technical requirements and content himself with moulding the two protrusions and their connecting duct into irregular ziggurats, whose rude and bulky forms

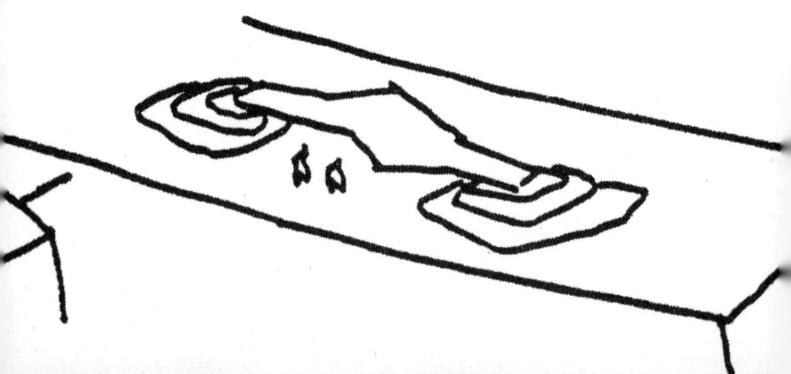

ill-accord with the relatively sophisticated character of the office block as a whole.[3]

But what exactly was supposed to happen here on the roof, when the PCF members came out to sit on these sprawling slabs? Since the headquarters also includes an elegant dining room, it was not necessary as a place to eat.[4] Perhaps it was just a spot for a cigarette break with an excellent view over the neighbourhood. Even so, we can imagine the comrades might have felt a bit awkward as they lounged on the garden's benches. Whereas Le Corbusier imagined his roof gardens as hoisting the green ground plane up into the air, and provided a mesmerising elevated landscape for strolling, the roof garden on place du Colonel Fabien seems to have been infiltrated by a piece of the old Barrière du Combat, with its staged animal fights: for what its chunky topographic contours invariably bring to mind are those engineered zoo landscapes that safely contain the animal kingdom's larger predators – polar bears, snow leopards, grizzlies, crocodiles and cougars – while evoking their natural habitat in an abstract way. Perhaps from the safety of place du Colonel Fabien, non-communist observers could occasionally catch a glimpse of a few of their human adversaries – planning, theorising, smoking – as they awaited the great moment of revolution from within this poured concrete roof habitat. What did the communists do to make this interminable wait bearable?

↗

Oscar Niemeyer, sketch of roof, 1967

If newer Parisian recruits could learn the main arguments that Marx levelled against Dühring, Feuerbach or Hegel over a desk in the basement meeting rooms or a table in the cafeteria, the building itself could also teach them Le Corbusier's five points of modern architecture. But beyond breaking the seal on the windows, is it possible for us to think of Niemeyer as parting ways with the established Corbusian language on place du Colonel Fabien? Not surprisingly, this larger relationship to Le Corbusier is a concern for Niemeyer himself in his memoirs. One subtle way the cosmopolitan architect seemed to feel he could step outside of the shadow of the over-sized Corbusian hand has to do, perhaps paradoxically, with the countries (and one country in particular) he was barred from, on account of his politics. This, then, is an extension of his previous political disagreement over whether architecture might change or be changed by life. 'Then I was invited to teach at Yale, but my visa application was denied; this went on for several years. Once when I was in Rome, I was again invited to the United States, so I applied for a visa at the local US embassy. Yet again, I was denied entry into the country, and I declared, "You know, I'm quite pleased with this. If you continue to refuse me a visa after 20 years, it means I haven't changed".'[5]

As convenient as it was for audiences in Europe and the United States to understand Niemeyer as more or less applying Corbusian ideas in a Brazilian context, and as useful as this frame was for his legibility, the kinky engineering and the engineering of kink also had something to say about moving on from Le Corbusier. Among these was the question of engineering in Niemeyer's work. As early as 1943, in the Church of St Francis of Assisi, Niemeyer dispensed with what had been the primary dualism of architectural structure: the opposition of the weight-supporting column and the heavy slab. By making the entire structure a concrete vault, this contrast disappears. Engineering often comes up as a point of pride in Niemeyer's writings: 'We were beginning to show the old world that there wasn't much they could teach us Latin Americans.'[6] And yet, what the old-world architects believed they had taught the Latin Americans was also, at moments, a point of contention. It takes a rather literal-minded, even obtuse viewer to notice none of the fantasy dimensions that attend Le Corbusier's buildings, and see them in terms only of his simplest press release statements, such as the functionalist proposition that a house is 'a machine for living in'. Machines *can* of course be kinky and excessive – as his always were. But because Le Corbusier was willing to float such statements about functionalism, we will at least grant this as a potential, if low-hanging, point of differentiation. But whether or not Le Corbusier was ever really a functionalist, there were such creatures, and some of them did have power, which they could deploy in snarling ways at the likes of Niemeyer. Max Bill, for instance, once described Niemeyer's buildings as 'an orgy of anti-social extravagance', working himself up into such a froth that his metaphors tripped over one another.[7]

Of his array of buildings at Pampulha, Niemeyer writes (with comparative calm): 'The project was an opportunity to challenge the monotony of contemporary architecture, the wave of misinterpreted functionalism that hindered it and the dogmas of form and function that had emerged, counteracting the plastic freedom that reinforced concrete introduced.'[8] Here, Niemeyer is taking an avant-garde dance step into the domain of the *moderne*, the mid-century built world of nocturnal pleasures that Sigfried Giedion, writing dismissively two decades later about recent American work, would name 'playboy architecture'.[9] It is difficult to wax earnestly and puritanically about the primary expression of function in a yacht club or casino, or in a covered platform designed for dancing next to a lake. In such spaces, as Niemeyer was quick to intuit and outfit, fantasy overtakes function.[10]

The curves Niemeyer used here and throughout his work have received quite a bit of attention, and even branding: the architect titled his memoir *The Curves of Time*. 'I was attracted by the curve – the liberated, sensual curve suggested by the possibilities of new technology yet so often recalled in venerable old baroque churches.'[11] But what, ultimately, is the effect of this curvilinear language? When the idea began to enter contemporary architecture, Niemeyer says, 'Le Corbusier alone refused to jump on the bandwagon. I remember him once remarking, "Oscar, what you are doing is baroque, but it's very well done".' And again, several years later, 'They say my work is baroque, too. But just look at that photo of the model for the Congress at Chandigarh – not everyone would do that.'[12] Le Corbusier seems to be asserting that however robust his curvilinear vocabulary, he cannot be summed up by this larger stylistic term. But Niemeyer pushes beyond the suggestion that Le Corbusier shared a baroque language with him: 'It was obvious that my architecture had influenced Le Corbusier's later projects, but this factor is only now being taken into account by critics of his work.'[13]

But mid-century neo-baroque was of course more than just an architectural language of curves. From roughly the 1920s until the moment of the PCF commission, the term was actively theorised by Latin American writers, among them Alejo Carpentier, José Lezama Lima and Haroldo de Campos, often in the context of post-colonial arguments.[14] For them, neo-baroque referred to a new world recoding of more than architectural conventions – an attempt to reframe and remobilise the aesthetics of colonisation, court spectacle and scientific instrumentalisation for other ends.

In the late 1960s and early 1970s, the exact period in which Niemeyer's building was realised, a new round of

theorisation of the term occurred in the work of a Cuban author living in France, Severo Sarduy, who proposed that it might be seen in explicit dialogue with structuralism. 'Baroque language' then becomes 'a turning back upon itself, the marks of its own reflection, the *mise-en-scène* of its own theatrical props'.[15] Like its more conventional usage, this new account built a bridge from the seventeenth century to the present, even if for Sarduy the relation was not exactly causal or sequential, but rather was associated with the term *retrombée*, which Alex Verdolini glosses as 'an echo – specifically, echoes of cosmological models in works of literature, art and architecture' and then links this term to three English concepts: 'fallout, upshot, feedback'.[16] In this sense, Sarduy equates the baroque of both the seventeenth and the late

Oscar Niemeyer at his Casa das Canoas, Rio de Janeiro, 1965

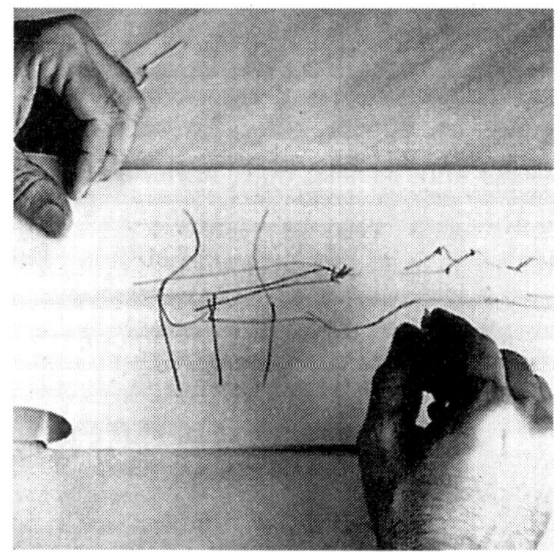

Still from a film in which Oscar Niemeyer draws his signature curves (above) and some of the typical sketches (below and overleaf)

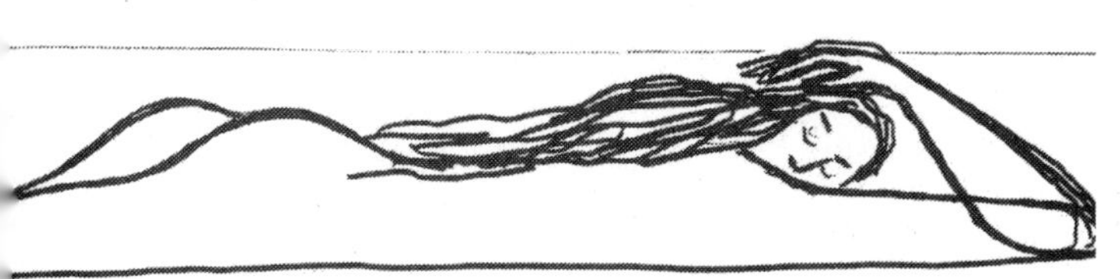

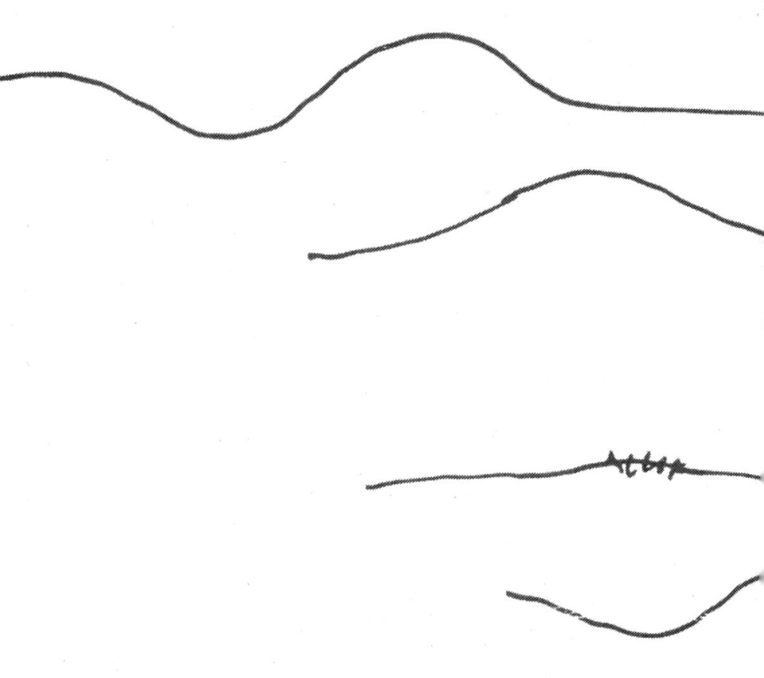

twentieth century with 'extravagance and artifice, perversion of a natural and balanced – moral – order'.[17] His more structuralist use of the concept – though underpinned by a social antagonism – is no longer primarily about the post-colonial, but about class, gender and desire more broadly: 'to be baroque today means to threaten, judge and parody the bourgeois economy, based on the stingy administration of goods, at its very centre and foundation'.[18] Such terms might link up well with Niemeyer's critique of functionalism and his pursuit of a bodily architecture: 'baroque space', Sarduy proposes, 'is the space of superabundance and squandering'.[19]

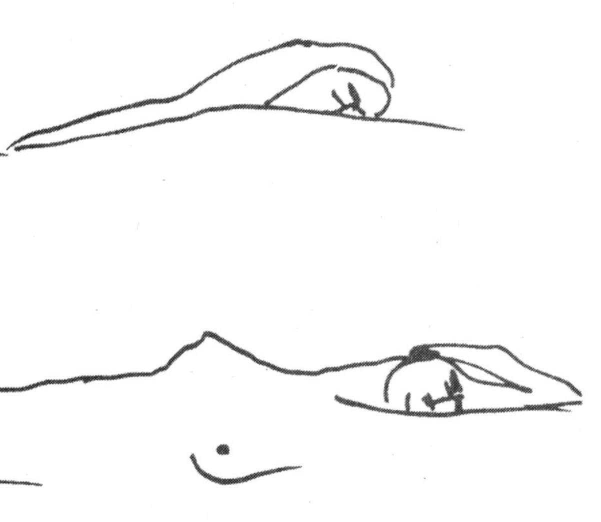

Though Niemeyer's practice may lodge desire more firmly in a heterosexual matrix, it seems that his use of the term baroque can be read not just as cultivating the curve in a generally corporeal sense, but as highlighting the curves of surprisingly specific bodies, and even of specific bodily parts. Indeed, in his memoirs, the word baroque applies equally to architecture and to bodies.[20] After noting that the city of Ouro Preto has some 'fine baroque buildings like their Portuguese counterparts',[21] he soon describes women he met in Porto Alegre: 'The girls were all shapely and pretty; they had the baroque buttocks that we favoured and a natural and homespun air.'[22]

Imagine Leonardo's Vitruvian Man or Le Corbusier's Modulor replaced by the rounded buttocks of a Brazilian woman. Imagine this last as the architect's fundamental diagram. For Niemeyer, such a bodily form, and the desire it initiates, is in fact the ground zero of architecture. An avowed atheist, he was nevertheless prepared to allow for a version of the Deus Artifex: 'I would say that it is a lubricious and imaginative being that impels us toward sexuality, architectural creativity and fantasy.'[23] To the degree that a creator exists, his role is to awaken sexual interests. He manages the universe by activating sexual pleasure. In addition to bodies that arouse desire, the lubricious creator also employs architecture and fantasy.

Critics might understandably bristle at the old-fashioned heterosexism of Niemeyer's cheeky cosmology. But the element of his baroque body aesthetic that is perhaps worth pausing on is that it is not simply an idealisation of the body in line with Greek or Renaissance Italian tastes. Rather, it is a contestation of those tastes, of those idealised bodies, with a different set of bodies that exaggerate one feature, the butt. Here, Niemeyer's humanism – at first glance timeless – runs up against history: 'This deliberate protest arose from the environment in which I lived, with its white beaches, its huge mountains, its old baroque churches and its beautiful suntanned women.'[24]

FANTASY AND COUNTER-FANTASY

The PCF building's language of desire and liberation depends not just on opening a window in the curtain-wall to breathe in the fine Parisian air, or going up to the roof garden to smoke and gaze happily over the neighbourhood. It also depends on being drawn into the orbit of the building's dome. And this occurs, first, in a ground-level garden that we have yet to explore with any thoroughness; a delay perhaps explained by the compromises that also attend it, in particular the installation of the fences that separate the space of place du Colonel Fabien from the original imagined entry sequence. But let's not reproach Niemeyer for events outside his control: if we were to enter the compound, as originally intended, at the corner of the square (the more leisurely and elegant of the two main entries), we would be greeted by a concrete paving surface that, in plan, presents a smaller and slightly more curving version of the circulation tower behind the office slab. It is framed against two patches of grass whose contours are partially edged by its continuation, now as a pathway that leads one first directly toward the dome, and then around it to the right, into the space of the plaza. All this is both biomorphic and painterly in plan. But the actual experience is more sculptural, since this sequence ensures not only that we contemplate the dome as a looming presence while we approach it head on, but also that it disrupts our path, making movement impossible unless we change tack and circle around it. Both the perception of sculptural mass from changing angles and the bodily adjustment to its path-blocking presence occur in a garden space that plays paving against planting while it gradually raises us to the top of the plaza.

By the time we reach the dome, our concrete concourse has risen one metre off the ground to the right and become a plinth; if we study the vertical surface, we notice a very narrow strip of windows serving a few of the subterranean secondary rooms. This subtle introduction to the underground prepares us for our plunge into the basement. Less micro-managed, perhaps, than the paving patterns that direct the steps around the front garden of the modernist house in Tati's *Mon Oncle* (1958), the path into the PCF headquarters is nonetheless programmatic. It is a baroque garden *soirée*: an organically shaped concrete walkway conducts us around sculptural domes, up against floating buildings and ultimately down a mysterious staircase into a communist netherworld.

In both its textual and bodily guises, baroque Brazilian counter-modernism might seem to clash with the neo-colonial agenda which works by proudly tracing the origins of all modernity back to Europe (as in Belmondo's encounter with a Corbusian building in Rio) or, in its less aggressive alternative, seeks to cleanse the history of compromised European forms by bathing them in the alternately innocent or politically radical atmosphere of the new world.

It is perhaps this latter strategy that is evoked by the opening credits for *L'Homme de Rio*, where a series of brightly coloured horizontal bands – yellows, blues,

---

Jacques Tati, Mon Oncle, 1958

JEAN-PAUL BELMONDO

DANS

L'HOMME

DE

RIO

greens, oranges, reds – rotate periodically to reveal more names, all to the soundtrack of a Brazilian drum riff (scored by the French composer, Georges Delerue). The language quietly suggests geometric modernism, but does so within a vivid new world palette. Again, as with Lévi-Strauss, we are seeing the immediate translation of an indigenous Brazilian visual pattern into a cosmopolitan French language. Though indigenous here also means modern – more so than with Lévi-Strauss's face paintings. Since these are the opening credits, it is through this very trope that we are invited to contemplate the narrative that follows.

Could Niemeyer's building in Paris be understood through a similar transcultural grid? If so, what was it that the French left saw in its curtain-wall and the pulsing white environment of the dome? At the most basic level, they saw Corbusian high modernism now recast as Marxist. But this was not simply European Marxism; it was also a Brazilian Marxism associated with revolution and post-colonial struggle in the so-called developing world. For such a translation to work, Niemeyer needed to galvanise his building's actors. As a substitute for the well-rehearsed, too familiar fantasy of the synthesis of the one and the many, the individual and the collective, a more specific fantasy, that of the heliotrope bending toward its light source, becomes attractive, even necessary. Granted, the curtain-wall building is less an individual flower and more a kind of elegant hedge. Some viewers might also question the cosmogenic powers of a sealed, underground dome – one

Opening credits, L'Homme de Rio, 1964

whose outer manifestation is not yellow, but white. And yet the basic ball and curved bar system of the building does invite a cosmological comparison, the linking of plant and sun, of a growing entity and an energy source. Moreover, the tilted concrete ground plane on which this composition sits, the garden-becoming-building, works to activate and organise the previously somewhat inchoate site.

Niemeyer himself did not propose plants or solar systems as part of the building's metaphorical structure. He called instead upon the human and the organic, suggesting that the dome of the PCF evoked the stomach of a pregnant woman (was he concerned that the austere communists might not appreciate a reference to the baroque buttocks he typically favoured?) Notwithstanding Niemeyer's statements, elaborate fantasies (the heliotrope among them) have been part of the building's afterlife; only they have come, in the main, from positions fundamentally hostile to the PCF headquarters' original purpose.

More particularly, as membership declined and the party became strapped for cash, PCF leader Robert Hue began to lease out the space for fashion shows – beginning with Prada in 2000.[1] But let us not pshaw at the irony without considering what this might actually mean. When Althusser alludes to a gap between an ideological representation and reality, we are likely to think of heroic socialist–realist modes in relation to abject poverty. But the afterlife of the PCF headquarters – when it began to be rented out as a stage-set for fashion companies, music videos and films – offers a more interesting and surprising version of this same problem.

Take the music video *La Jalousie* (2018) by the Belgian singer Angèle, in which a troupe of skinny models languorously clump around the green-carpeted basement before engaging in a range of vaguely post-Merce Cunningham movement routines on the tables of the assembly hall. Their claimed message? Consciousness, not structure: the private, inward pain of evil old jealousy, though this of course is used structurally to sell an entirely anonymous musical commodity that only simulates intimacy. Even here it's easy to approach this whole problem with an overly secure irony: one could note, for instance, that this commodification of Communist Party architecture has a basically contradictory relationship to the very ideals of the party. Privatisation of the public sphere, the use of a now 'exotic' and otherworldly environment to promote record sales – these are precisely the kinds of activity a Communist Party comes into being to contest. One could add that if a party cannot keep such images from circulating, then it is hardly likely to produce much change in the world. All still a bit too obvious. Perhaps a more interesting angle emerges when we ask of the party what sort of counter-image it offers; not simply modes of 'critique', but rather actual ideological images that could put this building to uses the party could endorse, a kind of ... spectacle, which even if structurally ideological, could at least broadcast attractive images of the daily life imagined by the party.

And so, we repeat the question: what are these images and how are you going to go about generating

---

Angèle, La Jalousie, 2018 (overleaf)

them? The upper echelons of the party are still thinking. Nothing immediately comes to mind, even though the elegant building in which they are housed could easily have helped them generate such fantasy scenarios. That is, generate their own fantasies, rather than allowing received, regressive ones to be staged on their home turf. Shifting their position on this problem would involve acknowledging, as Althusser suggested, that Marxists, too, produce ideology rather than simply manifesting class consciousness. Maybe this is the real failure, or at least a scene of struggle: the inability or unwillingness to construct a counter-image regime, a strategic ideology of, say, state-sponsored initiatives that extend from protection against predatory capitalism to real social and cultural initiatives, wage equity, immigration support and ecological activism – an image regime that is not afraid to look attractive, otherworldly, unfamiliar, and yet still be in some sense accessible, usable. What if all this was the real promise that had been forgotten in the building? What if the highest calling of the PCF headquarters was, as its enemies intuited, to operate as an evocative stage-set for the production of images? Would it not then be time to stop grumbling from the green-carpeted lobbies about pop videos made by their tenants and instead come up with their own, better ones?

In 2020, for the 85th edition of the annual leftist festival, La Fête de l'Humanité, the French Communist Party invited the electronica band La Fine Équipe to perform inside the dome. A film was made of the event. Now, it's true that an hour-long film of an electronica band performing under a dome may not seem to offer any immediately tangible image of the political concerns inventoried above. And yet the differences between this performance and that of Angèle do help to suggest what a progressive ideological campaign might ultimately look like: in the pop video, a star and her entourage of dancers use the dome and underground lounges for a performance that does not include an audience. The basic structure is hierarchical: the dancers are a foil for Angèle, and the dome and green chambers in turn operate as backdrops for both. Thematically, the music presents itself as a discourse on the dangers of jealousy, as it operates, implicitly, within a horizontal social world like that instantiated by the group of five dancers. But one can also say, without much cynicism, that the practical 'meaning' actually offered by the video is the distanced admiration of Angèle, as the apex of pop star perfection within a rarefied and glamorous world of high-end architectural surfaces

---

La Fine Équipe, La Fête de l'Humanité, 2020 (overleaf)

and young, perfect bodies. The jealousy her discourse would help us work through at the level of theme is thus reinstated by the very structure of the video itself.

In La Fine Équipe's performance, by contrast, four DJs spin and mix LPs at more or less the position a speaker for the PCF would occupy, under the folded

corner of the dome that operates as a stage. An audience is invited into the assembly hall to participate in the event; over the course of the set they rise from their seats and dance. A light show activates the space and connects the DJs, through various light geometries, to the rest of the hall, where the audience moves freely.

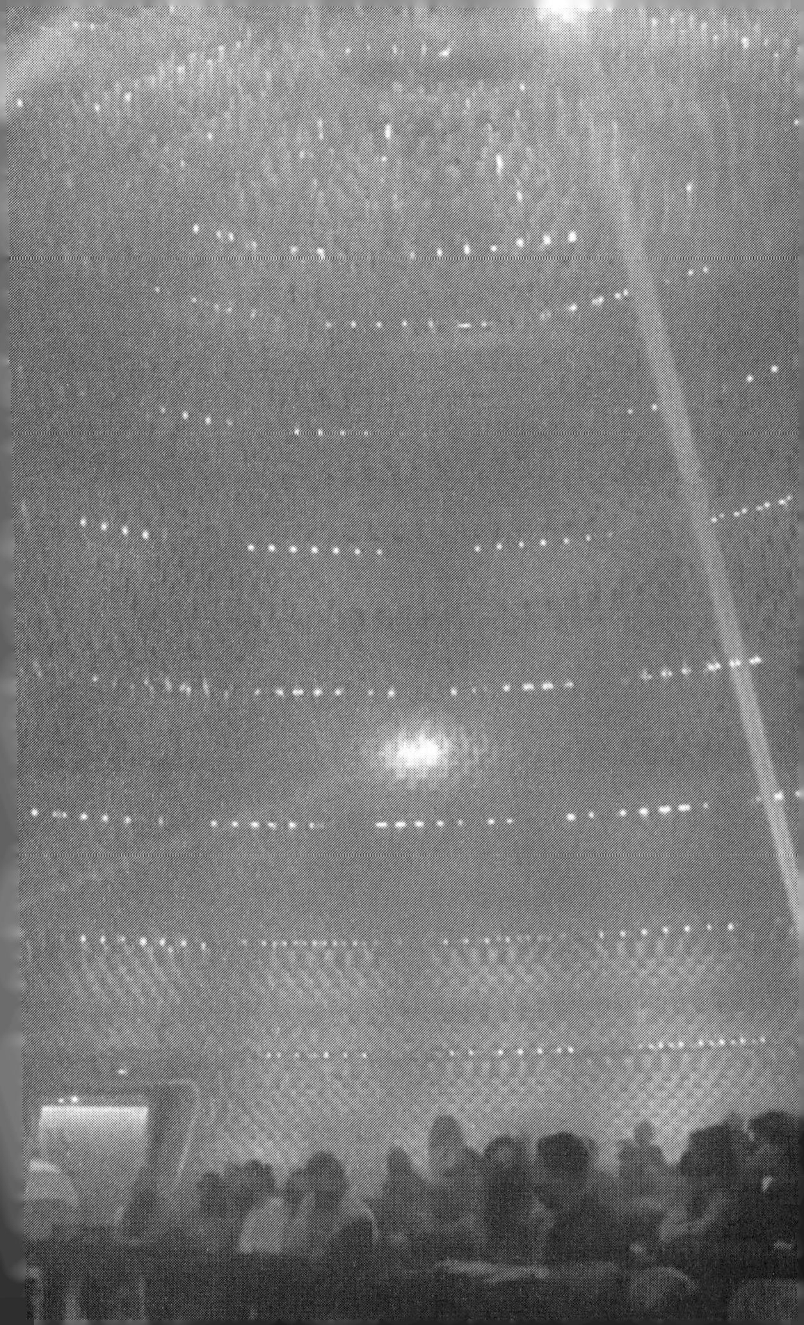

In this sense, the social space is far more horizontal: no one of the four DJs is in charge, and the group, in turn, at once energises and shares the space of the dome with the listeners. Then, turning to what we might call the 'content' of their music, another fundamental contrast becomes apparent. The raw material on which the music is based is mostly funk and pop from the 1960s and 70s, but this is reconfigured into a series of micro moments within riffs, drumbeats or vocal utterances as they are unfolded through processes of repetition and variation. In the process, La Fine Équipe locates a latency in these earlier recordings, treating them as mines for new rhythmic territories that emerge from, but ultimately change the terms of, this previous music. That they conceive of this practice as in some sense public and democratic may be suggested by the fact that one of the group's DJs goes by the tag Chomsky.

BRAZIL'S FRANCE

Niemeyer devotes a large part of his memoir, *The Curves of Time*, to his largely negative experiences with clients and contractors in Brazil. Of the hotel he designed in Ouro Preto, he writes: 'Israel [Pinheiro da Silva] had tried to help me by ordering repairs at the hotel but had not realised that the person chosen to carry them out did not measure up to the task. Things are so different in the old world! We still put up with such a lack of accountability here in Brazil!'[1] Niemeyer then immediately contrasts this with an episode from the construction of the PCF.

> Some years ago, in Paris, with the headquarters of the French Communist Party completed, Jacques Duclos, the general secretary of the PCF, called me to say, 'Oscar, the building is ready and it is very beautiful, but I have a request to make. I have here an old desk, one with a history of its own, it has been with me all my life.' He wanted to know if I would agree to place it in his new office. Now, that is real consideration for people! True respect for the work of others! When shall we hear of this happening in Brazil?[2]

If Duclos had called Niemeyer when the entire building was complete, and not just when the office slab could be occupied, it would have been 1980, some 15 years after the project was initiated. And however

The PCF building under construction, 1972

gracious Duclos might have been in deferring to the architect on the matter of office furnishings, the drawn-out process of construction complicates the contrast Niemeyer sketches. After the curtain-wall building was completed in 1972, there was a five-year hiatus while the party negotiated with a couple of adjacent property owners who refused to sell, blocking the excavation site of the dome. While part of this delay may have been attributable to the PCF's desire not to strong-arm their obdurate neighbours, such a timeline invited speculation about why the party most committed to the idea of the vast, world-building power of workers seemed incapable of organising its own works programme for a moderately sized building in a small part of the world. Then, after excavations began in 1977, the final section required an additional three years. At this point there might have been further speculation – also a bit

The PCF building with the auditorium dome still incomplete, 1978

ungenerous – about why the groundwork of the famous celebrants of the base seemed to elude the party.[3] Was there some embarrassing inefficiency or failure in planning (for which only the PCF could be responsible) that kept the proletarian subject of history sweating and huffing as he chipped rocks in an endless Parisian underground worksite?

Certainly, Le Corbusier, who devoted a high quotient of his tightly managed schedule to writing (and quickly publishing) treatises about efficiency, would have been horrified if one of his buildings had been held up in such a shameful manner. And yet it is also the case that, for all architects' bluster about developing better methods of building and working more generally, they must operate in political and economic contexts that they cannot control, contexts that flatten their intentions and 'abstract' their language into irritating pseudo equivalencies. If such engines of anonymity were capable of allowing doubts about the PCF's ability to embody party values during the construction process of its Parisian headquarters, they could certainly also render Niemeyer's and Le Corbusier's modernism practically interchangeable. And this imagined equivalence, as much as any whispering campaign about inefficiency, would have been a basic problem for the party.

Claude Lévi-Strauss interviewed by François Jacob on the French TV show Un certain regard, 1972

This is not to assume that understanding Niemeyer within a Corbusian frame is simply a given: only that it was so for these French intellectuals in the 1960s. The account they developed is interesting, then, not because it is the ultimate truth of Niemeyer's building, but because it tells us important things about Brazil's relation to France, about the PCF's shifting relationship to modernism and about architecture's possible relationship to structuralism.[4]

How, then, did the PCF explain their attachment to Niemeyer? First, given what we now know about the failure of the party to fight fantasy with fantasy, it seems fair to assume that Niemeyer's critique of functionalism and cultivation of playboy modernism was not a central selling point for the French Communist Party. PCF members had not turned to Niemeyer because his buildings in Pampulha, for instance, had put them in touch with new desires they could articulate collectively: to samba under the wavy ceilings of the restaurant and dance club; to sip caipirinhas behind the *brise-soleils* of the yacht club, before sailing across the lake and meeting one's baroque-figured girlfriend for a tryst at the still empty Church of St Francis of Assisi. Nor could this woman's curvy buttocks be presented as a new world subversion of the gangly figure of Le Corbusier's Modulor man. Whatever these French leftists may have felt individually, this was not the story they could use to explain their attachment to Niemeyer. Yes, a few members might have been excited about his claims to have pushed engineering farther than Le Corbusier ever did, but were such ambitions clearly manifested in the PCF building? To most eyes, it would not have seemed to offer any kind of structural advance over the Salvation Army Building or the Unité in Marseille.

Could we perhaps borrow a trick from Lévi-Strauss's structuralism here and shift the plane of analysis from the would-be inherent meaning of an individual element of culture to the larger systems of oppositions in which such an element can take on meaning, through contrast? That is to say, if the 'language' of Corbusian modernism didn't have so much of an inherent meaning, but rather took on contextual meaning, perhaps something important happened when it was used by a South American leftist to design a Communist Party headquarters in Paris?

In a remarkable passage in *Tristes tropiques*, Lévi-Strauss offers a dense synthesis of his conclusions about the function of Caduveo face painting. But his observations might equally well apply to the Parisian communists' need for an exogamous architectural commission. As he writes, 'The inbreeding practised by the castes [read: 'French intellectual life'] and the ever-increasing gradations in the hierarchy must have made it more difficult to have marriages [or in this case 'architectural commissions'] that corresponded to the concrete necessities of collective life. This alone can explain the paradox of a society being opposed to procreation and, in order to safeguard itself against the dangers of improper alliances within the group, having recourse to a form of inverted racialism through the systematic adoption of enemies or foreigners.'[5]

Granted, the PCF isn't so much opposed to procreation as simply having a hard time generating new members. Despite the pregnant woman symbol of

A Caduveo dome, photographed by Claude Lévi-Strauss (above), and the dome of the PCF building (below)

Indigenous Cashinaua boys from Peru reading Tristes tropiques, photo David Allison

their dome, the reproduction of communists in Paris has stalled. And yet communism in the Global South is on the rise. As a prominent Brazilian communist, Niemeyer is obviously not an 'enemy', though he is a foreigner. Design, here, is a way of reconciling a pallid reality with the more robust category of the potential.[6] Here is Lévi-Strauss once more:

> But the remedy they failed to use on the social level, or which they refused to consider, could not elude them completely; it continued to haunt them in an insidious way. And since they could not become conscious of it and live it out in reality, they began to dream about it. Not in a direct form, which would have clashed with their prejudices,

> but in a transposed, and seemingly innocuous, form: in their art. If my analysis is correct, in the last resort the graphic art of the Caduveo women [read: design of Oscar Niemeyer's PCF headquarters] is to be interpreted, and its mysterious appeal and seemingly gratuitous complexity to be explained, as the phantasm of a society ardently and insatiably seeking a means of expressing symbolically the institutions it might have, if its interests and superstitions did not stand in the way.[7]

The point is not that the PCF wants simply to be Corbusian; it's that it wants to be modernist but at the same time distance itself from the social meaning of architectural modernism in France as it was developed by Le Corbusier. The Parisian communists believe that turning to a South American modernist with leftist politics might achieve this. But they must repress the fact that Niemeyer's formation was Corbusian and – to the degree that he broke out of that formation – his post-functionalist politics of architectural fantasy were illegible to them, as they were deemed irresponsible by the PCF. This is the 'superstition' on which Lévi-Strauss concludes; the fear of pleasure and improvisation that made the party look backward to the generation of 1968.

In this way, the PCF is both haunted by and attracted to the dream that its building might be an erotic heliotrope. But such an identification would undermine the traditional political aesthetics to which it still clings, despite compelling new challenges from Althusser, the French New Wave, Deleuze and Guattari and others. And so PCF members must instead see their undulating glass and concrete home within more familiar modernist rhetorics of functionalism and transparency which make it increasingly indistinguishable from the work of the villain of the piece, Le Corbusier. Is not this failure of imagination at least partly responsible for condemning the party and its gorgeous building to the role of historical monuments, rather than engines of contemporary political change?

But perhaps such a position leaves us stranded in the familiar territory of the aesthetic as ideology: the imaginary compensation for real loss. The actual losses for the Communist Party during this period make such a relationship hard to avoid entirely. But looking at the problem through the famous Parisian treatise on Indigenous Brazilian structuralists might add nuance. Earlier we examined a passage from *Tristes tropiques* in the context of *L'Homme de Rio*, where it was imagined to gloss the backstory on the Malket Indigenous Indians. But read it now, if you will, as an account of Niemeyer's clients on place du Colonel Fabien.

> The fact is that these primitive people, the briefest contact with whom can sanctify the traveller, these icy summits, deep caverns and impenetrable forests – all of them august settings for noble and profitable revelations – are all, in their different ways, enemies of our society, which pretends to itself that it is investing them with nobility at the very time when it is completing their destruction, whereas it viewed them with terror and disgust when they were genuine adversaries.[8]

'Primitive' because the communists do not accept the supposed inevitabilities of the modern economy. 'Enemies of our society' for more obvious reasons. Whether we're 'investing them with nobility' is a moot point, but we can agree that we're 'completing their destruction'. Though PCF members certainly imagined a robust future for their party in 1965, the end of the Cold War introduced a radically different narrative. Today, most would be inclined to see communists as something of an exotic and endangered life form.[9]

However it is perceived, the Communist Party seems to have lost. Its attempts to contest capitalism's most basic assumptions and structures – especially its claims to self-evidence and universality – were met, not with the condescension shown toward the Caduveos, but with terror, disgust and violence. What is poignant about this situation is that, unlike the Caduveos, these European primitives did have real power across the twentieth century – a real shot at pulling off a fundamental change in the structure of world societies, though their time, too, seems to have come to an end.

When the whole building officially opened in 1980, European communism was depleted, in its final decade as anything other than a theoretical position. Historians and anthropologists could study its past, but expansion plans would not be realised. Now, perhaps, there was a slightly sentimental pause as the glowing orb that once pulled in heliotropes finally sank below the horizon. On his long voyage to the new world, anticipating his future objects of ethnographic inquiry, Lévi-Strauss practises description on the sunset in a way that might help us understand the setting sun of the PCF building as it passes into structuralism's version of night, with its play between always enticing individual singularity, and always knowable larger pattern.

> In the direction of the sun, a new bar now rose up behind the previous one, which had hardened into a uniform, confused cement block... Nothing is more mysterious than the series of always identical but unpredictable processes by which night follows day. Its marks appear suddenly in the sky, attended by uncertainty and anguish. No one can foresee the form that the resurgence of night will adopt on this unique occasion.[10]

DOUBLE REVERSE

A rookie detective might try to conclude here on Lévi-Strauss's beautifully painted twilight, with his object of enquiry reversed, applied not to Caduveo face painting in Brazil but rather to the problem of how Parisian intellectuals could deny Corbusian modernism while embracing a nearly identical aesthetic, now deemed authentic because it was associated with a Brazilian architect with impeccable leftist credentials. But such a reading still presents us with a number of problems. First, it partakes of that I-know-you-are-but-what-am-I logic by which anthropology has been imagined by some of its less generous auditors to discourse, always and only, about its observers and not its ostensible objects of analysis. Ironically, it is perhaps the famous Brazilian interpreter of Lévi-Strauss, the anthropologist Eduardo Viveiros de Castro, who most forcefully makes this very point about anthropology. As he proposes in his book, *Cannibal Metaphysics*: 'By always seeing the same in the other, by thinking that under the mask of the other it is always just "us" contemplating ourselves, we end up complacently accepting a shortcut and an interest only in what is "of interest to us" – ourselves.'[1] *Anti-Narcissus* (the Brazilian brother of *Anti-Oedipus*) was to have been the name of the treatise that would diagnose and transcend this problem in part by reframing Lévi-Strauss, who 'deserves to be credited not only with having re-founded [the human sciences] with structuralism but also with virtually "un-founding" them by pointing the way toward an anthropology of immanence'.[2] What Viveiros de Castro proposes, in other words, is that by the time of Niemeyer's commission, in 1965, the French anthropologist was in fact no longer a structuralist, having shifted from the properly structuralist terms of *The Elementary Structures of Kinship* (1949) and even *Tristes tropiques* (1955) to the emergent post-structuralism of the four volumes of *Mythologiques* (1964–71).[3]

Where this is of particular epistemological use for Viveiros de Castro is in a turn away from the human as the ultimate organising category. In postulating *Anti-Narcissus* as his great unwritten work, Viveiros de Castro is obviously not trying simply to salvage old-fashioned descriptions of other cultures. The issue, in other words, is not merely that anthropologists who

Claude Lévi-Strauss in his office at the University of São Paolo, c 1938

look at their ethnographic objects see only themselves. It's also that what they see is conditioned by their a priori assumption that their objects of analysis will, paradoxically, offer a fundamental contrast to their own being: they will be non-occidentals, non-moderns and even non-humans. This last is perhaps the most important and surprising category that enables Narcissus and requires his critique. As he puts it: 'If a subject is an insufficiently analysed object in the modern naturalistic world, the Amerindian epistemological convention follows the inverse principle, which is that an object is an insufficiently interpreted subject. One must know how to personify, because one must personify in order to know.'[4] Rather than venture deeper into the intricacies of Viveiros de Castro's enticing and influential posthumanism, let us just note here that, strange as it seems, it is a Brazilian interpreter of the purportedly post-structural Lévi-Strauss who makes the most powerful case for why anthropology might be something more than a projection, so long as it also involves a turn away from our tired humanism toward an actual curiosity about the non-human world.

Where, then, does that leave the reversal of object proposed with *Tristes tropiques*? To believe that a few of its richest passages might also describe the problem of how Parisian intellectuals selected a Brazilian architect to design the French Communist Party headquarters, we need not succumb to the model of a purely narcissistic anthropology that can only characterise its own observing subject. Like the windows of the PCF building, oscillating between reflection, opacity and transparency, the intricate texture of Lévi-Strauss's prose in *Tristes tropiques* might reveal a subcurrent of reflexive commentary on his own culture that supplements rather than obliterates its ostensible project of describing a real situation in Brazil. For is it not the case that the PCF – shrinking in power and prestige, and eager to appeal as both 'open' and connected to revolutionary struggles throughout the world – found itself forced into 'the systematic adoption of ... foreigners' when selecting an architect to design its new Parisian headquarters? And is it not also the case that Niemeyer's break with functionalism – with the French modernist architecture that the party distrusted – coincided with his cultivation of a series of erotic propositions that the PCF could never quite publicly admit, which became 'the institutions [the party] might have, if its interests and superstitions did not stand in the way?' And did all this not contribute to the continual marginalisation of this political movement, especially after 1968, to the extent that we now encounter these 'enemies of our society' in the 'deep caverns' of their communist cave, as objects of historical and even natural historical curiosity?

FINAL GROUNDING

In Lévi-Strauss's description of twilight, 'a new bar [rises] up behind the previous one, which had hardened into a uniform, confused cement block'.[1] This image may point to the darkening horizon, to the lights going off in the PCF building in Paris. But it also points to something important about the tilted ground plane of the front plaza. On a recent visit to the site, it seemed possible to see this plane differently: for all the potential problems Niemeyer generated by sinking the programme underground, the sloping concrete of the front plaza is still more than just an organic foil for the dome that bulges out of it. As we know, this was a move Niemeyer underlined in his sketches, by drawing orthogonal options which he then crossed out. Constructivist buildings like Melnikov's had proposed that their own tilted planes and rotated axes were, in some basic way, celebrations of the human power to control the physical and material conditions in which subjects live and work. Grid shifts in plan, torques to elevation, seemingly arbitrary roof angles – all these denaturalised forms could be equated with the revolutionary project of denaturalising capitalist relations, and taking control of history, of the physical and social envelope in which we operate.

Niemeyer doesn't use diagonals or grid shifts to do this, but his language at place du Colonel Fabien might be seen as a kind of organicist constructivism: what appears to be the given ground plane, the base and point of departure for a world, is here totally controlled, and turned into an elegant human construction. As it sweeps up from the public square to the curtain-wall building, it suggests both that a ground can be made (and not merely received), and that a building like this, which posits its dome as a kind of sun and its office bar as an orbiting set of planets, can operate as an alternate cosmology, a quiet reminder about the negotiable and buildable character of the seemingly given. Visiting the building with me, John Melillo, a literary critic and musician, suggested that we see the curtain-wall building as the crest of a wave now breaking onto the city, a kind of communist tsunami always about to impact the world via place du Colonel Fabien. Even the tilt of the ground plane works with this reading, since waves pull water up into their vertical surface. But as much as one might want to believe this, it feels as if the symbolism has been reversed, and it was communism that was being hit by a wave. A wave of common sense, of practicality, of market logic. Not a wave that denaturalised anything. But one that set the ground plane 'straight' again. Fixed it. Corrected it.

One afternoon, while working on this project, I took the metro out to St Denis to visit Niemeyer's late building for *L'Humanité*, the organ of the PCF and historically the most powerful communist newspaper in France. The newspaper still organises, every September since 1930, the largest annual leftist gathering in the country, Fête de l'Humanité Paris: 'three days of festivities, with thousands of people embracing each other in solidarity and browsing the stands as if a brave new world was already beginning!.. I had never seen anything like it anywhere', is how Niemeyer himself described it.[2] And yet, even though it's located in the reddest of the red Parisian suburbs, the paper has struggled to survive in its new building since day one.

Niemeyer's office for *L'Humanité* was completed in 1989, not an auspicious year for communism, and things have only gotten worse. It sits, now in a terrible state of disrepair (comparable with Niemeyer's more neglected Brazilian buildings), across a small park from the great cathedral of St Denis, the first crystallisation of the gothic. Its plan is a kind of bent-Y with its base pointing at the church's famous choir. A few of the details in the history of this light-filled structure, and the debates in which it was embroiled, might, as they say, illuminate the last steps of our path.

In Erwin Panofsky's account, Abbé Suger was concerned to use his now-canonical writings about his

Oscar Niemeyer, L'Humanité building, Paris (below and overleaf)

patronage of St Denis to rebut charges of materialism.[3] When his more austere contemporaries criticised the lavish rebuilding of the abbey church, Suger insisted that precious materials were the very means of transporting a 'dull mind' to a higher plane: 'The process by which the emanations of the Light Divine flow down until they are nearly drowned in matter and broken up into what looks like meaningless welter of coarse material bodies, can always be reversed into a rise from pollution and multiplicity to purity and oneness', he writes.[4] Or, as Panofsky puts it, 'Instead of turning his back on the physical world, [man] can hope to transcend it by absorbing it.'[5]

Parlaying the Cistercians' critique of Suger's materialism into an ostensible demonstration of its opposite at St Denis, employing the overdetermination of flying buttresses to help distribute the weight of taller walls more thoroughly dissolved into glass, this was not just a local success.[6] St Denis' claim to absorb and transcend materiality, then, as Stephen Murray puts it, 'lies at the heart of French cultural identity – with "nation" and "gothic" architecture emerging not just in the same place and time but also in immediate relationship. With St Denis, gothic emerges as the logical expression of *le génie français* and the creation of a society unified under monarch and church.'[7] This sense of unity is produced by the newly physical experience of light in gothic churches, which in turn is enabled by the building's larger, more prominent windows, which in turn are made possible by the emergence of flying buttresses. These, as mentioned earlier, distribute the task of support between two systems or, as Althusser would say, 'overdetermine' that support.

How, then, might Suger's project relate to those of his newer neighbour in St Denis and the PCF headquarters on place du Colonel Fabien? In one sense, both Marxist discourse and architecture ought to provide a neat inversion of what gothic was taken to achieve, and what Suger did in his writing: Marxists want their critics, want their contemporary Cistercians, to understand their building projects as thoroughly materialist. Perhaps a good Marxist building, like the larger discourse to which it is connected, could offer ways of grounding abstractions, of siting and framing immaterialities within everyday life.[8] But could a well-realised

Marxist structure, like Niemeyer's headquarters, really be thought of as a materialisation of the abstract? Could such a project even focalise a place and time?

In exploring the mystery of Niemeyer's communist cave this investigation has tried to suggest some of the ways in which the building's basic charge – representing the Communist Party in the Paris of the 1960s – can help us think, in surprisingly concrete ways, about some of the underlying problems of Parisian political aesthetics in that period. Here, the building has prompted us to reimagine the relations between concepts and expanses of poured concrete, between political programmes and the architectural language of curtain-walls and plans, between the statements or opinions of an individual architect and the complex histories of architecture institutionalised through books and exhibitions. But it is difficult to say that the PCF building itself operates as a tool for grounding abstractions. Better to say that it provides an occasion, and a context, for us to do so.

Now, it is almost certainly true that, despite our best efforts, Niemeyer's building still lacks the Marxist Suger who could ghostwrite its project, situating the PCF headquarters in the kind of compelling materialist discourse that might unify the party, the country and even its new world allies. Though this may sound like an excuse, part of the problem that attends the composition of such a definitive defence stems from the ambiguous status of the term 'materialism', both

---

Oscar Niemeyer, photographed in his Mondadori Palace building, Segrate, Italy, 1975

generally and perhaps especially within Marxist discourse.[9] Materialism, like modernism, is now a plural phenomenon – and rightly so. Compelling attempts to 'materialise' have benefitted from a wider sense of what might rightfully count as matter: in addition to the matter of the economy that has often monopolised the term 'historical materialism', we also have the matter of language and its displacements, of the body and its desires, the atom and its swerves, and, increasingly, the physical world and its temperatures. If any new development could increase membership numbers at the PCF, it would most likely be this last materialism of the warming world, since whatever reservations one may harbour about Marxism, its alternative has proved especially skilled in continuing to heat seas, lakes, air and soil, and thus at not so gradually snuffing out the possibility of life on this large planet – a deadly enough 'contradiction' that we may be forced to update Deleuze and Guattari's seemingly long valid dicta that contradictions don't necessarily lead to social change.

And yet, these emergent uncertainties around the constitution of matter might also highlight elements of idealism in classical Marxist thinking: for all of Marxism's 'materialism', temporally it requires a basic negation of the here-and-now in order to cultivate a fundamentally different time to come that since 1989 has slipped farther and farther into a fictive future.[10] It's here, then, that Marxism meets the future-oriented narrative dimensions of Christian other-worldism. If ambitious architecture always proposes a world of which it is an anticipatory fragment (even when we encounter its language at a long historical remove, so that it cannot help but become an antiquated futurism), then this problem gets interestingly compounded in a Marxist structure, for which the future is not merely the enticing cosmology imagined by the visionary architect, but also a fundamentally different set of economic and social relations that would, as it were, secure and institutionalise the functioning of that cosmology, but which architecture itself has but the tiniest say in determining. Unlike a transient political action, the multivalent body of the person who performs it, or even the comparatively inconspicuous paper or book that contains a Marxist manifesto or treatise, a Marxist building (in Western Europe at least) cannot help but loom into prominent quasi-permanence only to remind you of its not quite being there, at least in the way that it wants to be there, as the full realisation of its aspirations. In this sense, even the best finished Marxist building – like Niemeyer's in Paris – is always, a priori, a construction site.

What perhaps newly came to characterise such a site in the Paris of the 1960s, then, was the slowly dawning sense that, however fundamental, the pending transformation that would ultimately complete the site was not a 180-degree turn from falsity and ideology to truth and class consciousness – not an orthogonal, right-angular relationship, but a curved and oblique one, if you will. The fantasy surplus or the projected desires that attended images of party positions would not simply vanish in the air with the successful revolution, but would necessarily remain, in a minor form, in representations offered by the party, including the building of the party itself. But what also came newly to characterise such communist construction sites in the 1960s was the beginning of the end of the Cold War. The questions, then, were not just what the party might do with its new theories of ideology and representation, but also, alas, what an emboldened, post-Cold War West might do with the representatives of its communist parties.

Maybe the sun darkened on place du Colonel Fabien not just because Niemeyer decided to enclose the assembly hall underground. Maybe the long night that has descended on this heliotropic structure is also historical and, as Althusser would say, overdetermined. His theory of how political regimes retain control suggests a link, as we've seen, to the emergence of the gothic at sites like St Denis, with its use of two systems to support the cathedral's upper storeys: load-bearing walls and flying buttresses. For Althusser, this architectural metaphor helped explain how exactly societies were kept in check: since the threat of violence was not quite enough, this threat went hand in hand with the quieter work of cultural institutions like schools and museums, as they embody and explain culture. This work extended to criticism more broadly, including the book you have in your hand. Althusser, in this sense, developed an early understanding of the arts as affecting rather than merely reflecting politics.

But maybe overdetermination might help us understand not just how governments retain control, but also how they gradually come apart. For if contradictions could lead to fundamental changes in the present, it seems likely that they will not be purely economic (despite what Marxists have long asserted), but rather economic–ecological. This last development (the end of the world) may be the most hopeful sign on the horizon for the PCF. But I will not take you, reader, into a more concrete imagination of the likely apocalypse, and of Marxism's slim chances of helping us avert it. Instead, in looking at the moment of the emergence of structuralism, I've sought merely to follow one literal Marxist structure, one elegant party headquarters in the nineteenth arrondissement, through the recent intellectual and social history of Paris, and its points of contact across the globe, especially Brazil. This has taken me from the Mato Grosso to the Museé de l'Homme, from popular to avant-garde films, through histories of sites and political parties, and from official architectural discourses to a range of more experimental approaches. I've tried to trace out the string of fantasies associated with the Parisian PCF building: those floated by the architect, developed by the party, brought in by renters of its spaces, and, most of all, those latent in the still articulate structure. That the building's horizons of possibility have narrowed since its moment of conception in 1965 strikes me not so much as a failure of Niemeyer's imagining of the future. Rather, it seems both the result of the obvious historical decline of communism and the less obvious failure of imagination of the left: the Fine Équipe concert notwithstanding, the party has been unable to counter the capitalist fantasies enacted by those who hire the building's spaces with equally powerful leftist ones, generated by or staged within the very same building.

Could these fantasies, well staged, have slowed or even reversed the party's decline? It's hard to say. What seems clearer, and what this book proposes – somewhat uneasily between history and theory – is that when the PCF was forced to search its shrinking coffers for resources and imagine how to move forward, it could have done more with the latent knowledge that its building is a valuable stage. And rather than simply renting out that stage to the party's enemies, it could have used it as a launch pad for reclaiming some power in the present and the future, even if that power now only operates at the scale of a neighbourhood heliotrope. But such mysterious cosmologies may be due for a quiet reappraisal. For whatever else the yearly warming sun makes us feel, it's likely to encourage us to feel a bit differently about alternatives to the heavy, if invisible, hand that keeps turning up the broiler; in which case Marxism, for all its warts and creases, may get another look. And in that scenario, Niemeyer's building in the nineteenth arrondissement in Paris will be a good place to start looking.

THE CALL OF THE DOME

1. Le Corbusier died the year of Niemeyer's commission and so could never have seen the building, and is of interest here, anyway, less for his own judgements than for the judgements against him by the French left.
2. See for instance the 2013 documentary film, *The French Communist Party's Headquarters*, by Richard Copans and Stan Neumann.
3. The catalogue is *Oscar Niemeyer: Textes et Dessins Pour Brasília* (Paris: Éditions Forces-vives, 1965).
4. Oscar Niemeyer, *The Curves of Time: The Memoirs of Oscar Niemeyer*, translated by Izabel Murat Burbridge (London: Phaidon, 2000), 105.
5. Perhaps the most influential critique of the PCF position in 1956 was Jean-Paul Sartre's series of articles, 'Le Fantôme de Staline', published that year and the following in *Les Temps Modernes* (129–31). This appeared in English as *The Ghost of Stalin,* translated by Martha H Fletcher (New York: Braziller, 1968). For a defence of the party see Irwin W Wall, 'The French Communists and the Algerian War', *Journal of Contemporary History*, July 1977, 521–43.
6. Niklas Maak, 'The Curves of Life: An Interview with Oscar Niemeyer', in *Oscar Niemeyer: A Legend of Modernism* (Basel: Birkhäuser, 2003), 24.
7. Niemeyer, op cit, 163.
8. He was to collaborate with two French architects: Jean Deroche and Paul Chemetov (both PCF members). It was finally, Vanessa Grossman explains, the party treasurer, Georges Gosnat, who (along with Jean Nicolas) seems to have made 'the party's final decision for Niemeyer, and afterwards for his old friend Prouvé. Since the prewar years Nicolas, who was also close to Charlotte Perriand and Le Corbusier, played an important role in promoting modern architecture before the PCF, in particular, and the left in general' – Vanessa Grossman, 'Niemeyer's Headquarters for the French Communist Party, 1965–1980', in Regina R Félix and Scott D Juall (eds), *Cultural Exchanges Between Brazil and France* (West Lafayette: Purdue University Press, 2016), 166.
9. Sherban Cantacuzino, *The Architectural Review*, March 1972, 143. Though construction of the PCF building ran all the way from 1967–80, the offices were complete by 1972, when this part of the building was reviewed (quite positively) both by Cantacuzino and in an unsigned editorial by the magazine in that same issue. The point about the hammer and sickle is not directly from Cantacuzino, however; he merely notes that this had been remarked in a previous review in *La Nouvelle Critique*.

10. From the beginning, the building has been understood in relation to Le Corbusier: writing of the strategy of placing a sculptural object in front of an office bar, *The Architecture Review* notes that 'This is a well-tried formula, first stated in 1930 by Le Corbusier in his Pavillon Suisse, of a tall slab contrasted with a low-lying and freer form', Cantacuzino, op cit, 134. The same review concludes that Niemeyer's is 'probably the best building in Paris since Le Corbusier's Cité de Refuge for the Salvation Army'. In perhaps the most substantial monograph of the architect, Styliane Philippou stresses the Corbusian dimensions of the building's appearing to float: 'The plaza pavement peels off the ground and curls up where it slots under the main block, veiling the sturdy columns of the pilotis along the central longitudinal axis and allowing the undulating volume to appear to levitate weightlessly above the ground, pushing the Corbusian "clean line of the underside of a building" to new limits', Styliane Philippou, *Oscar Niemeyer: The Curves of Irreverence* (New Haven: Yale University Press, 2008), 328.
11. The question of Le Corbusier's politics has become a heated topic of late. For an overview of the recent literature, one might consult Simone Brott, 'The Le Corbusier Scandal, or, was Le Corbusier a Fascist' (*Journal for Comparative Fascist Studies* 6, 2017, 196–227. In this piece, Brott concentrates on three main recent monographs: Marc Perelman, *Le Corbusier: Une froide vision du monde: Essai* (Paris: Michalon Éditeur, 2015); François Chaslin, *Un Corbusier: Fiction & Cue* (Paris: Seuil, 2015); Xavier de Jarcy, *Le Corbusier, un fascism français* (Paris Albin Michel, 2015).
12. Like Brasília, Chandigarh was an explicitly post-colonial government, in this case commissioned by Nehru.
13. That said, Le Corbusier's rush to offer himself to the Vichy government does deserve some underlining, although it's unlikely that Marxists in 1965 would have been fully aware of this oily chapter in Le Corbusier's life, since the architect was in fact quite successful at air-brushing over his activities during the Second World War. See Nicholas Fox Weber, *Le Corbusier: A Life* (New York: Knopf, 2008), 413–69.
14. Many writings on Niemeyer make this point, and an unsigned review of this particular building also underlines the relationship: 'Remembering Le Corbusier, Niemeyer has transformed the roof garden-terrace into a "promenade architecturale" shaping the two towers (containing the conditioning plants), as tiered pyramids and linking them as a sort of bridge', *Domus* 511, 1971.
15 Grossman, op cit, 165.

1. Note that the theft occurs during a quaint, old world lunch break, during which the museum actually closes and, right in the gallery, the guards sit down to an ample spread, including both a large bottle of wine and a round of camembert, which both of the guards sniff for quality assurance. Indeed, it is precisely the guards' attention to the details of their table that allows for the theft upstairs.
2. The shopping malls at Orly Sud were, in fact, so popular that the airport became, in the early to mid-1960s, the second most visited site in Paris, behind the Eiffel Tower. French film viewers would be treated to a more extended consideration of the site three years later in the opening section of Jacques Tati's *Playtime* (1967).
3. Niemeyer, op cit, 86.
4. Or that was his official story anyway; in an interview, Maak asks: 'Though you have always referred to yourself as a communist, you built the barracks and army HQ for the dictatorial regime under Medici. (Niemeyer ignores the question)', Maak, op cit, 24.
5. Niemeyer, op cit, 61. And yet, like the experience of Claude Lévi-Strauss in Brazil, something about his time in Brazil seems to have stuck with Le Corbusier. Even late in life, one of Le Corbusier's (many) eccentricities was, according to Weber, the architect's insistence upon carrying a large Brazilian coin in his pocket, 'treating it as an icon, although it regularly tore holes, which a furious Yvonne [Le Corbusier's wife] then had to sew up', Fox Weber, op cit, 548.
6. Kenneth Frampton, *Labour, Work and Architecture: Collected Essays on Architecture and Design* (London: Phaidon, 2002), 223.
7. Ibid.
8. Stamo Papadaki, *Oscar Niemeyer* (New York: Braziller, 1960), 14.
9. Museum of Modern Art press release; the exhibition was also supposed to demonstrate the influence of the 'free form shapes' of Jean Arp on the landscape design of Niemeyer's collaborator, Roberto Burle Marx. The show ran from 15 February to 17 April 1949.
10. After hurling the plans down the stairs, the architect bellows: 'I want windows everywhere. Don't hesitate to make it transparent... This building should be like a dragonfly wing.'
11. This claim has been more or less accepted by most of Niemeyer's critics: Philippou, for instance, proposes that Brasília involved 'the second discovery of Brazil, by the Brazilians themselves', Philippou, op cit, 215. See also David Underwood, *Oscar Niemeyer and Brazilian*

Free-Form Modernism (New York: Braziller, 1994).

12. Among other sources see Isabel Löfgren, *Satellite Lifelines: Media, Art, Migration and the Crisis of Hospitality in Divided Cities* (Amsterdam: Institute of Network Cultures, 2020).
13. Maak asks: 'You recently visited Brasília again for the 40th anniversary celebrations. Would you build it like that again?' To which Niemeyer responds: 'Yes. The cathedral and the Plaza of the Three Powers I would. But the city has become ugly, it has no uniformity, there is no beauty in the new satellite towns. The people that live there are poor but it is not a question of good or bad architecture. That is a question of politics', Maak, op cit, 22–23.

COMMANDING THE DOME

1. In describing the dome's situation, Philippou also compares the element to a spacecraft: 'The only source of natural light, a glazed strip around the opaque auditorium dome, draws the visitor towards the skewed, dramatically lit, white walls of what looks like a spaceship that has pierced the ground and landed on the green carpet. The spacecraft theme continues in the airlock-like doors and other futuristic details of the auditorium', Philippou, op cit, 329.
2. Outer space does make an appearance in Niemeyer's memoirs. Of his friend Joaquim Cardozo (an engineer and architect who worked on Brasília), Niemeyer writes: 'I recall the countless subjects we discussed... At times Cardozo would step out on the veranda in our office, look up at the sky, and declare, "We must get to the observatory!" That would be the beginning of long conversations about stars, infinite space, distant nebulae and the grandeur of the universe', Niemeyer, op cit, 64.
3. As he puts it in his memoirs: 'Foreign countries are home to some of the best projects I have designed, namely the French Communist Party Headquarters; Bobigny's Bourse de Travail building; the Cultural Center of Le Havre; the FATA Office in Turin; the Mondadori headquarters in Milan; and the universities of Constantine and Algiers, in Algeria', ibid, 174.

THE ELEMENTARY KINSHIP OF STRUCTURALISTS

1. Claude Lévi-Strauss, *Tristes Tropiques*, translated by John and Doreen Weightman (New York: Atheneum, 1973), 175.
2. Among the many commentaries on the book, Clifford Geertz describes it as a 'moiré' com-

prised of: 'A travel book, even a tourist guide, if, like the tropics, out of date. An ethnographic report, founding yet one more *scienza nuova*. A philosophical discourse, attempting to rehabilitate Rousseau, *The Social Contract*, and the virtues of the unpetulant life. A reformist text, attacking European expansionism on aesthetic grounds. And a literary work, exemplifying and forwarding a [symbolist] literary cause', Clifford Geertz, *Works and Lives: The Anthropologist as Author* (Stanford: Stanford University Press, 1988), 44.

3. There is thus a dimension to Lévi-Strauss's discourse that could be compared to the other famous Martinican critiques of French education, offered by Aimé Césaire in *Notebook of a Return to the Native Land* and Frantz Fanon in *The Wretched of the Earth* – who must also unlearn and exteriorise their educations to proceed with the development of their thinking.
4. Lévi-Strauss, op cit, 41.
5. This latter building appeared in Godard's *Alphaville*, and was in that sense something of an exception within the filmmaker's larger pattern of attention to the architecture of the *banlieue*.
6. Grossman, op cit, 166, notes that the PCF was 'highly proud ... of the transparent [quality of the] six-storey office block'. In a dossier produced by the party, Gosnat claimed that 'For the first time in the history of our country, a party makes of its headquarters a house of glass', ibid. But given that such a statement might characterise only the office slab, and not the large proportion of the programme buried under ground, it seems inadvisable to let such a press release stand in for a full analysis of the headquarters as built.
7. Cantacuzino, op cit, 144.
8. Ibid.
9. Unsigned editorial, *The Architectural Review*, March 1972, 134.
10. See Michael Dennis, *Court and Garden: From the French Hotel to the City of Modern Architecture* (Cambridge: MIT Press, 1988).
11. Or rather, there were to have been more of these geometric abstractions until the building lost a floor, which means that most of the published plans are of the proposed rather than the as-built state.
12. Niemeyer, op cit, 174.
13. Philippou, op cit, 329.
14. Jean-Paul Sartre, 'France: Masses, Spontaneity, Party' in *Between Existentialism and Marxism: Sartre on Philosophy, Politics, Psychology and the Arts*, translated by John Matthews (New York: Pantheon, 1974), 124.
15. Ibid, 124–25.
16. Ibid, 120.

17. Even Le Corbusier would employ such a metaphor. Less than a year before rushing off to declare his desire to build for Vichy, he wrote: 'In France it is the peasant who holds the secrets of the race. In the harmonious construction called France, the land and its cultivation provide the fundamental economic, social and cultural foundation', Fox Weber, op cit, 410.

GOTHIC OVERDETERMINATION

1. Louis Althusser, 'Ideology and Ideological State Apparatuses' in *Lenin and Philosophy and Other Essays*, translated by Ben Brewster (New York/Delhi: Monthly Review/Aakar, 2006), 90.
2. Ibid, 124.
3. This occurred in part because, unlike almost all other building programmes from the period, St Denis's was managed by someone, Abbé Suger, who wrote copiously about his activities, if still not as much about the specific architectural character of his interventions as one might like. St Denis's central status was also aided by the fact that the father of iconography, Erwin Panofsky, happened to be the person who not only translated the medieval text, but also offered an extensive commentary, in which he called the building the 'parent monument of all gothic cathedrals' – *Abbot Suger on the Abbey Church of St Denis and its Art Treasures*, edited, translated and annotated by Erwin Panofsky (Princeton: Princeton University Press, 1979), xi. The first edition of this text was published in 1946.
4. Le Corbusier, *Towards a New Architecture,* translated by Frederick Etchells (New York: Dover, 1986), 74.
5. Ibid, 1.
6. Ibid.
7. Ibid, 47–48.
8. Perhaps the structural opacities produced by this extensive basement give us another way to understand the building's pilotis: thicker but more isolated structural elements became necessary once Niemeyer decided to house a large component of the building underground in what the architect referred to as a 'workers' lounge'.
9. It is remarkable that at no point during his excellent book on New Babylon – *Constant's New Babylon: The Hyper-Architecture of Desire* (Rotterdam: Witte de With, 1998) – does Wigley critique or even address the fallacy that with increased technology labour would disappear.
10. It is worth noting that the most evocative theorisations of artificial landscapes – Constant's and Rem Koolhaas's theory of 'Manhattanism' in *Delirious*

New York – were both conceived by Dutch architects who themselves grew up in the artificial landscape of Holland, whose fabrication was not so much depicted as re-enacted by the Dutch republic's most interesting landscape painters in the seventeenth century: Jan van Goyen, Jacob van Ruisdael and Meindert Hobbema.

11. I address the whole problematics of equating architectural and political 'transparency' in 'Nominal Transparency: Siting Government in Ireland', *The Global South*, Spring 2016, 56–84.
12. Wigley's reading of the problem of transparency in Constant's models of New Babylon provides a useful contrast: 'The modern architect's obsession with a radical transparency that exposes all the details of structure and lifestyle turns into an amorphous sense of between lifestyles too complex and transitory to be simply exposed. Clear shapes behind glass give way to a mysterious flickering glow. Transparency is put at the service of mystery', Wigley, op cit, 50–51.
13. *Philosophy of the Encounter: Later Writings, 1978–1987*, edited by François Matheron and Oliver Corpet, translated by G M Goshgarian (London: Verso, 2006), 268.
14. Karl Marx and Friedrich Engels, 'The Manifesto of the Communist Party', in Robert C Tucker (ed), *The Marx-Engels Reader* (New York: Norton, 1978), 473.
15. Ibid.
16. At one point in his memoirs, Niemeyer aligns this Marxist dynamic explicitly with the power of paper, but in the PCF building, it might also have to do with the concretising power of the architect's favourite material, concrete: 'Paper is the weapon of long-suffering people – those individuals who rise up against the injustice of life... It was on a sheet of white paper that Karl Marx announced a new world, which a privileged minority insists on postponing endlessly', Niemeyer, op cit, 148.

TRACKING SHOT I

1. The name comes from Denis Forestier, a student who led a drive for negotiations with the FLN.
2. Althusser had come up explicitly in Godard's film as early as *La Chinoise* (1967), when Jean-Pierre Léaud's character, asked about thinking in Europe that might supplement Mao, mentions that 'there's a great Althusser text about a Brecht play', before adding, 'I've made it mine'.
3. Ironically, Godard's credentials were such among leftists that he was able to get Fonda and Montand to commit to acting in the film for 'for no fee upfront

and a share of the profits', from Colin MacCabe, *Godard: Portrait of the Artist at Seventy* (New York: FSG, 2003), 232.

4. As MacCabe claims of Godard's works with Gorin, 'the whole thrust of the analysis is that it is impossible to "see" a social situation', ibid, 229.
5. This appears in a 1972 French documentary, *La Politique et le bonheur: Georges Kiejman,* directed by Patrick Camus.
6. By simpler he presumably means in relation to the hand-held cinematography of his earlier films, which tends to shift its point of view more frequently.

TRACKING SHOT II

1. This detail appears in the Copans and Neumann film cited earlier.
2. Its symbolism was lost neither on Victor Hugo, who includes a cameo in *The Hunchback of Notre-Dame* (1831), nor on Alexandre Dumas, who mentions it in *La Reine Margot* (1845). The structure is also briefly described in Luc Sante, *The Other Paris* (New York: FSG, 2015), 56.
3. Anthony Vidler, *Claude-Nicolas Ledoux: Architecture and Utopia in the Era of the French Revolution* (Basel: Birkhäuser, 2021), 107.
4. Louis Sebastien Mercier, *Panorama of Paris,* translated by Helen Simpson, edited by Jeremy Popkin (University Park: Pennsylvania State University Press, 1999), 48.
5. Vidler, op cit.
6. Ibid, 116.
7. Ibid.
8. Le Corbusier published a polemical book to coincide with the exhibit, *The Decorative Art of Today*, translated by James Dunnett (Cambridge: MIT Press, 1987) in which he first expands the concept to include all tools (or as he puts it, 'the totality of human-limb objects', 67) and then shrinks the concept to exclude decoration: 'Modern decorative art is not decorated', 81.
9. It was, then, between 1942 and 1965 that the site operated, in some capacity, as a labour union, though the main headquarters of the party was in the 9th arrondissement on rue Le Peletier. What is clear is that whatever building was on the site did not occupy the entire footprint of the current building, since it was the refusal to sell a couple of the houses that remained on the site that delayed the construction between 1972 and 1977, during which time it was necessary to enter the building through the emergency exit.
10. As biographer Fox Weber explains, the site given to Le Corbusier by the committee was an intentionally bad one; they were embarrassed by his building. Many trees (which the architect was forbidden from touching) were on the site,

which was 'tucked into the garden between the two wings of the Grand Palais', Fox Weber, op cit, 220.

11. While the 1925 plan stratified the classes, Le Corbusier's 1935 Ville Radieuse was the first of his urban plans to be organised by the size, not the income, of the families housed there.
12. Weber, for instance, fundamentally doubts that the architect intended the plan literally: 'he did not intend for it to be followed. He neither imagined it really would be done nor thought it should be', ibid, 218.
13. On Le Corbusier's work in the USSR, see Jean-Louis Cohen, *Le Corbusier and the Mystique of the USSR: Theories and Projects for Moscow, 1928–1936* (Princeton: Princeton University Press, 1992).

POST-HUMANIST STRUCTURES

1. Philippou writes of the 'endearing gentleness' of the dome as it pokes through the ground, and of its 'becoming an ordinary, even humorous, object, seeking attention, keen to participate in the everyday life of the city – not a perfectly shaped Platonic volume suggesting a long pedigree which PCF might not have wanted to evoke', Philippou, op cit, 328.
2. Maak, op cit, 25.
3. Niemeyer, op cit, 169.
4. While Niemeyer mentions the importance of his having read Sartre (after which, he 'viewed life as an unfair and unrelenting tragedy' (ibid, 163), there is no indication that he read Césaire or Althusser or any of the post-structuralist theorists.
5. Philippou, op cit, 90.
6. This is how György Lukács articulates this distinction: 'By relating consciousness to the whole of society it becomes possible to infer the thoughts and feelings which men would have in a particular situation if they were able to assess both it and the interests arising from it in their impact on immediate action and on the whole structure of society. That is to say, it would be possible to infer the thoughts and feelings appropriate to their objective situation'. György Lukács, *History and Class Consciousness*, translated by Rodney Livingstone (Cambridge: MIT Press, 1971), 51.
7. To a degree, Althusser here replays the problems generated by a moment when Marx writes, in his critique of Hegel, 'Life is not determined by consciousness, but consciousness by life', in Tucker, op cit, 155.
8. Ibid, 233.
9. Ibid.
10. The critique was mutual. As Barry Bergdoll explains in his essay 'Learning from Latin America: Public Space, Housing and Landscape': 'For US and European critics, Latin American

architecture was haunted by the spectre of individualism, which challenged the ideal of modernism as a universal and communal project', in Barry Bergdoll, Jorge Francisco Liernur and Patricio del Real (eds), *Latin America in Construction: Architecture, 1955–1980* (New York: Museum of Modern Art, 2015), 21.

11. 'His vision was of an architecture destined to establish a kind of visual mythology for Brazil, superseding all the architectural myths that preceded it. In this sense, Niemeyer's oeuvre holds the position of founding fiction', Philippou, op cit, 90.
12. Ibid. Already in his 1960 monograph on the architect, Stamo Papadaki writes of the 'acceptance of the non-functional as a legitimate architectural task' and of an 'architecture of pleasure', Stamo Papadaki, *Masters of World Architecture: Oscar Niemeyer* (New York: Braziller, 1960), 21–22.
13. We know that Niemeyer would sometimes use his sketches in this kind of polemical way. 'Every time I designed a curved block standing alone on a site, for instance, I presented it with accompanying sketches showing that the existing curved topography had suggested it', Niemeyer, op cit, 170.

POST-STRUCTURALIST MARX

1. As Dominick LaCapra writes of one prominent example: 'Sartre sees structuralism as an analytic, neopositivist methodology that denies the importance of human praxis in history. "Structure" is for him an acceptable notion only as it designates the moment of the practico-inert in a more comprehensive dialectical process', preface to Dominik LaCapra, *Sartre* (Ithaca: Cornell University Press, 1978), 233.
2. Until now, Lévi-Strauss has been presented more or less as the inventor of structuralism. But this is certainly incomplete: the anthropologist himself credited Roman Jakobson with making him aware of the almost unconsciously structuralist dimension of his early work, a dimension that, in Jakobson's writing, was already fully self-conscious and articulate. Of his meeting with Jakobson, Lévi-Strauss says in an interview with Didier Eribon: 'At the time I was a kind of naive structuralist, a structuralist without knowing it. Jakobson revealed to me the existence of a body of doctrine that had already been formed within a discipline, linguistics, with which I was unacquainted. For me it was a revelation', Didier Eribon, *Conversations with Claude Lévi-Strauss*, translated by Paula Wissing (Chicago: University of Chicago Press, 1991), 41.

3. Eric Drott, 'Rereading Jacques Attali's *Bruits*', *Critical Inquiry*, Summer 2015, 726.
4. Ibid, 731.
5. Ibid, 734.
6. Ibid, 747. Drott offers a bigger picture history of the fallout of 1968 within the field of music in Eric Drott, *Music and the Elusive Revolution: Cultural Politics and Political Culture in France, 1968–1981* (Berkeley: University of California Press, 2011).
7. This comes up in the unsigned *Architectural Review* editorial in 1972: 'Although the decision to build was taken before the 1968 elections (at which the party lost 40 seats) the new headquarters may also be seen as an act of consolidation, a bold and imaginative gesture which the leadership believed to be necessary at a time when the party's political fortunes stood at a low ebb', op cit, 133.
8. Gilles Deleuze, *Difference and Repetition,* translated by Paul Patton (New York: Columbia University Press, 1994), 10.
9. Gilles Deleuze and Felix Guattari, *Anti-Oedipus: Capitalism and Schizophrenia*, translated by Robert Hurley, Mark Seem, Helen R Lane (Minneapolis: University of Minnesota Press, 1985), 120.

POST-CORBUSIAN BAROQUE

1. As Le Corbusier puts it: 'Every country builds its houses in response to its climate. At this moment of general diffusion, of international scientific techniques, I propose: only one house for all countries, the house of exact breathing. The Russian house, the Parisian, at Suez or in Buenos Aires, the luxury liner crossing the equator will be hermetically sealed. In winter it is warm inside, in summer cool, which means that at all times there is clean air inside at exactly 18 degrees. The house is sealed fast! No dust can enter it. Neither flies nor mosquitos. No noise.' Cited in Dean Hawkes, *The Environmental Imagination: Technics and Poetics of the Architectural Environment* (London: Routledge, 2008), 33.
2. One measure of how widely accepted air-conditioning was at the time is the fact that Constant's New Babylon was to have been air-conditioned. See Wigley, op cit, 10.
3. Cantacuzino, op cit, 144.
4. Although, as Cantacuzino notes: 'The self-service canteen on the sixth floor was a failure from the start because French administrators, whatever their creed, insist on being served at table', ibid, 144.
5. Niemeyer, op cit, 89.

6. Ibid, 95.
7. Maak, op cit, 22.
8. Niemeyer, op cit, 62. Similarly, of Brasília: 'it was no longer the imposition of the right angle that angered me, but the obsessive concern for architectural purity and structural logic, the systematic campaign against the free and creative forms that attracted me and which were viewed contemptuously as gratuitous and unnecessary', ibid, 171.
9. Sigfried Giedion, *Space, Time and Architecture* (Cambridge: Harvard University Press, 1967), xxxii. He continues: 'an architecture treated as playboys treat life, jumping from one sensation to another and quickly bored with everything. I have no doubt that this fashion born out of an inner uncertainty will soon be obsolete; but its effects can be rather dangerous, because of the worldwide influence of the United States', ibid.
10. To his credit, Papadaki registers this problem in the first monograph on Niemeyer. 'Modern architecture, until then concerned with the health, the rational comportment, of man and his physiological needs – fresh air, sunshine and contact with nature – had remained aloof from man's night life', Papadaki, op cit, 20.
11. Niemeyer, op cit, 62.
12. Ibid, 63.
13. Ibid.
14. De Campos, for instance, includes Niemeyer's buildings in Pampulha in his account of the neo-baroque.
15. Severo Sarduy, *Barroco and Other Writings*, translated by Alex Verdolini (Stanford: Stanford University Press, 2025), 35.
16. Ibid, xviii.
17. Ibid, 30.
18. Ibid, 74.
19. Ibid.
20. It can also occasionally apply to prose style, as for instance when he describes the nineteenth-century Portuguese novelist Eça de Queiroz as 'at times baroque, though full of wit and spontaneity', ibid, 43.
21. Niemeyer, op cit, 41.
22. Ibid, 54.
23. Ibid, 6.
24. Ibid, 170.

FANTASY AND COUNTER-FANTASY

1. Thom Browne and Jean Paul Gaultier also had exhibitions there. The 2013 film *Mood Indigo* (based on a Boris Vian novel) was shot in the building; a series called *Osmosis* was also recorded there, as were several videos, including one by the French singer Alain Souchon, and another by the Belgian singer Angèle.

BRAZIL'S FRANCE

1. Niemeyer, op cit, 59.
2. Ibid.
3. And yet, the finished headquarters was by no means dismissed, either because of its extended construction process or for its outcome. Indeed, even Georges Pompidou praised the building, describing it as 'the only good thing those commies had ever done', ibid, 96.
4. More recent work on Brazilian architecture has tended to move away from its relation to Le Corbusier. In an essay comparing the architecture in São Paulo with that in Rio de Janeiro, for instance, Carlos Eduardo Comas proposes that for both 'brilliant relatives included Le Corbusier, but it would be a mistake to overestimate his influence on the highly educated Brazilians architects. Corbusian references were important, but they were only one kind among many. Moreover, from the beginning these multiple references included Brazilian work itself, past and present, erudite, vernacular or utilitarian', Carlos Eduardo Comas, *Latin America in Construction*, op cit, 62.
5. Lévi-Strauss, op cit, 195.
6. As Barthes had put it, 'the basic operation of criticism is the uncovering of myth posing as nature, that is, the self-interested historical operations of one class presenting themselves as the timeless unfolding of human existence. The institution of French Marxism, that is, bears a basic, structural relationship to the question of myth', Roland Barthes, *Mythologies*, translated by Annette Lavers (New York: Noonday, 1990).
7. Lévi-Strauss, op cit, 196–97.
8. Ibid, 41.
9. As Niemeyer puts it: 'joy and sorrow are our old and inseparable companions and, with a smile, I see that communism has not died, as they have tried to tell us', Niemeyer, op cit, 142.
10. Lévi-Strauss, op cit, 67.

DOUBLE REVERSE

1. Eduardo Viveiros de Castro, *Cannibal Metaphysics*, edited and translated by Peter Skafish (Minneapolis: University of Minnesota Press, 2017), 41.
2. Ibid, 46.
3. *The Raw and the Cooked* (1964); *From Honey to Ashes* (1966); *The Origin of Table Manners* (1968); *The Naked Man* (1971).
4. Ibid, 62.

FINAL GROUNDING

1. Lévi-Strauss, op cit, 67.
2. Niemeyer, op cit, 86.
3. These charges came not so much from Bernard of Clairvaux himself, with whom Suger had made peace in 1127, but rather

with a larger emergent culture of 'Cistercian puritanism', Panofsky, op cit, 26.

4. Ibid, 19.
5. Ibid.
6. Panofsky does not discuss St Bernard's other writings, but one can imagine Suger fastening onto the claims of a sermon like 'On Conversion', for instance, which was preached probably at Notre Dame, after which Bernard took his converts to St Denis. See Bernard of Clairvaux, *Selected Works*, translated by G R Evans (New York: Pauline Press, 1987), 65.
7. Stephen Murray, *Plotting Gothic* (Chicago: University of Chicago Press, 2015), 75–77.
8. Certainly, this was one of the most powerful dimensions to Marx's own discourse: that of concretising or literalising those elements of his adversaries' arguments that often passed, abstractly, as common sense or accepted euphemism.
9. That materialist and idealist (or we might call them neogothic) projects are often, in practice, not quite so diametrically opposed can be seen in charges against many Marxists that their a priori commitment simply causes them to ignore or fundamentally mischaracterise salient historical realities. This, for instance, was Lévi-Strauss's response to the charge that he ignored history: 'When Marxists or neo-Marxists attack me for not knowing history, I answer, "You are the ones who don't know it or are turning your backs on it, since in place of history you set up grand developmental laws that exist only in your minds"', Eribon, op cit, 125.
10. Niemeyer writes of this problem: 'The years went by. I witnessed the Soviet crisis and the collapse of the communist world, but I remained unchanged, convinced that what had happened could somehow be explained, something that the old Soviet communists would be able to clarify. I was mystified; I felt that my political position was not consistent with the events taking place in Brazil and in the world. Many people accepted the communist defeat as a consequence of old and irreparable mistakes, and quite a few others took it calmly, since it was what they had wanted all along. I refused to adopt those attitudes. I began to see the Soviet crisis as a natural phase of the political struggle, since humanity still had not reached the level that a communist society, united in solidarity, demanded', Niemeyer, op cit, 165.

ACKNOWLEDGEMENTS

Thomas Weaver helped this book's realisation on all fronts. I am also grateful to Merritt Bucholz, J D Connor and Edward Eigen for their comments on earlier drafts of the manuscript; to Pamela Johnston for her copy-edit; Colette Forder for her proofreading; Claudia Caranfa for her cover; Emma Brown for her image research; Verena Andric at Park Books for assisting with image rights; Teresa Lima and Adrien Vasquez for the book's graphic design; and to Françoise Fromonot for her encouragement and photographs. For conversation, suggestions and support during the process I am indebted to Jean-Philippe Antoine, Emily Apter, John Melillo, Lisa Robertson, Meredith Tenhoor, Sonali Thacker and Robert J C Young. For institutional support I owe thanks to my deans and chair at New York University – Elizabeth McHenry, Una Chaudhuri and Jenny Mann – and to the NYU Global Research Initiatives in Paris and in Berlin, where I am indebted to Nathalie Gicquel and Gabriella Etmektsoglou respectively. I dedicate this book to the two people who taught me the most about French thought: Jonathan Culler and T J Clark.

IMAGE CREDITS 4–5 © Guilhem Vellut/Wikipedia Commons; 10–11 © Laura Fantacuzzi & Maxime Galati-Fourcade/Cortili; 13 © Michel Moch; 15 © Farabola/Bridgeman Images; 16–17 © Marcel Gautherot/Instituto Moreira Salles Collection; Oscar Niemeyer/© 2026, ProLitteris, Zurich; 18 © Michel Moch; 20 © Jack Nisberg/Roger-Viollet; 21 Wikipedia Commons; 22–23 Oscar Niemeyer; 24 Wikipedia Commons; 25 Thomas Weaver; 27 © UN Photo; 30–31 © Haywood Magee/Getty Images; 33–36 Philippe de Brocca, *L'Homme de Rio*, 1964; 37 © Farabola/Bridgeman Images; 38 © Earl Leaf; 39 Philippe de Brocca, *L'Homme de Rio*, 1964; 40–41 © FLC/2026, ProLitteris, Zurich; 42 Le Corbusier, *La Maison des hommes*, 1942; 46–53 Oscar Niemeyer/2026, ProLitteris, Zurich; 44–45 © FLC/2026, ProLitteris, Zurich; 44–49 Philippe de Brocca, *L'Homme de Rio*, 1964; 50 *Revista Brasília*, no 39, 1960/Arquivo Público do Distrito Federal; 50–51 Philippe de Brocca, *L'Homme de Rio*, 1964; 54 Wikipedia Commons; 55 © Thibaud Poirier; 56–57 © Darren Bradley; 58–64 © Thibaud Poirier; 66–67 © Grant Smith/SuperStock; 68 © Louis Monier/Bridgeman Images; 70–71 © Grant Smith/SuperStock; 73 © Agencia Estado; José Moscardi; 75 © Apic/Getty Images; 76–77 Courtesy Princeton University Library; 79 Claude Lévi-Strauss, *Tristes tropiques*, 1955; 82 © UN Photo; Universidad de Alicante; 83 © Anne Salaün/Roger-Viollet; 84–85 Oscar Niemeyer/2026, ProLitteris, Zurich; 86–87 © Françoise Fromonot; 88, 91 © Thibaud Poirier; 92–93 © Anton Bucich; 96–97 © Laura Fantacuzzi & Maxime Galati-Fourcade; 98–99 © Thibaud Poirier; 100–101 Laura Fantacuzzi & Maxime Galati-Fourcade; 103–05 © Anton Bucich; 106 Jacques Tati, *Playtime*, 1967; 109 © Denis Esakov; 110–111; © Alain Mingam/Gamma-Rapho via Getty Images; 115 Wikipedia Commons; 116 Le Corbusier, *Vers une architecture*, 1923; 117 Wikipedia Commons; 120 © Françoise Fromonot; 121 © Constant Nieuwenhuys, *Sector Construction New Babylon*, 1966, photo Tom Haartsen/Pictoright Amsterdam 2026; 123 © Laura Fantacuzzi & Maxime Galati-Fourcade; 124–25 © Thibaud Poirier; 126–28 © Laura Fantacuzzi & Maxime Galati-Fourcade; 129 Wikipedia Commons; 130–31 © Denis Esakov; 134 Jean-Luc Godard, *Une femme est une femme*, 1961; Jean-Luc Godard, *Le petit soldat*, 1963; 135 Jean-Luc Godard, *À bout de souffle*, 1960; 136–39, 142–43 Jean-Luc Godard, *Tout va bien*, 1972; 146 Wikipedia Commons; 148 © Look and Learn/Bridgeman Images; 149–50 Wikipedia Commons; 151 © NPL – DeA Picture Library/Bridgeman Images; 153–55, 159, 160–61 Wikipedia Commons; 164, 166–67 © UN Photo; 168 Wikipedia Commons; 169 © Kurt Hutton/Getty Images; 172–73 Oscar Niemeyer/2026, ProLitteris, Zurich; 178–79 © Denis Esakov; 180 © Françoise Fromonot; 182–83 Wikipedia Commons; 186, 188–89 Chris Marker, *Le fond de l'air rouge*, 1976; 192–93 © Laura Fantacuzzi & Maxime Galati-Fourcade; 194 © Anton Bucich; 196–99 © Denis Esakov; 200 © Laura Fantacuzzi & Maxime Galati-Fourcade; 201 © Denis Esakov; 202 Oscar Niemeyer/2026, ProLitteris, Zurich; 204–07 © Laura Fantacuzzi & Maxime Galati-Fourcade; 211 Wikipedia Commons; 212 © Farabola/Bridgeman Images; 213–15 Oscar Niemeyer/2026, ProLitteris, Zurich; 219 Jacques Tati, *Mon oncle*, 1958; 220 Philippe de Brocca, *L'Homme de Rio*, 1964; 224–26 Angèle, *La Jalousie*, 2018; 228–31 La Fine Équipe, La Fête de l'Humanité, 2020; 234 Vanessa Grossman and Benoît Pouvreau, *Oscar Niemeyer en France*, 2021; 235 © Daniel Simon/Gamma-Rapho via Getty Images; 236 László Ruszka/INA via Getty Images; 239 Claude Lévi-Strauss; Michel Moch; 240 © David Allison; 246 Wikipedia Commons; 251–52 © Denis Esakov; 255–56 Mondadori Portfolio/Bridgeman Images; 262–63 © Guilhem Vellut/Wikipedia Commons; 280–81 © Denis Esakov; back cover © UN Photo

A NOTE ON THE TYPE

The *Gumshoe* series is typeset in Aluminia, a 2017 revival by Jim Parkinson of W A Dwiggins' Electra (1935). As Dwiggins tells it, with characteristic idiosyncrasy, Electra emerged out of a series of conversations he had with the spirit of the first-century Buddhist monk, poet and calligrapher, Kōbō-Daishi, in which the Japanese master first upbraided him for his unhealthy obsession with Renaissance typography and then encouraged him to instead pursue more contemporary allusions, and more specifically 'electricity… sparks, energy… high-speed steel… metal shavings coming off a lathe'. Electra is the result of these prompts, even if Dwiggins, self-critically, admitted that 'I can't quite see the metal shavings part'. Aluminia is the name of a foil-covered marionette Dwiggins made in the 1930s and Parkinson's revival type is named after her. To help Dwiggins liberate himself from more classical references, in *Gumshoe* Aluminia is paired with that most contemporary of sans-serif fonts, Futura (used for the captions, sub-headers and footers), designed by Paul Renner in 1927 and produced by the Bauersche Gießerei type foundry in Frankfurt.

The typeface used for the title and author's name on this book's cover is a variation of Pump, a font designed at precisely the same moment Oscar Niemeyer's Communist Party building was emerging from the ground by the English typographer Bob Newman. Pump was produced by Letraset, the dry-transfer lettering system, but somewhat unexpectedly, a version was also used for the opening credits of the original 1979 Russian release of Andrei Tarkovsky's *Stalker*, customised with Cyrillic accents and occasional slices through the letters themselves. Inspired by this assimilation, our version – adapted by Adrien Vasquez and renamed Gump – adds additional cuts and Russified letter inversions in keeping with the book's mystery.—*Thomas Weaver*

Mysteries of a Communist Cave
Lytle Shaw

A Gumshoe book

Concept: Françoise Fromonot and Thomas Weaver
Text editing: Thomas Weaver and Pamela Johnston
Proofreading: Colette Forder

Design: Teresa Lima and Adrien Vasquez,
Lima Vasquez studio
Cover art: Claudia Caranfa
Printing and binding: Nørhaven, Denmark
Prepress: farbanalyse, Cologne

Park Books AG, Niederdorfstrasse 54, 8001 Zurich, Switzerland
www.park-books.com
T +41 44 262 16 62
E info@park-books.com

Product Safety
Responsible person pursuant to EU Regulation 2023/988
(GPSR): GVA Gemeinsame Verlagsauslieferung Göttingen
GmbH & Co KG, Post Box 2021, 37010 Göttingen, Germany
T +49 551 384 200 0
E info@gva-verlage.de

Park Books is supported by the Federal Office of Culture
with a general subsidy for the years 2021–2025.

ISBN 978-3-03860-447-1

Coming soon!

GODZILLA AND THE TEMPLE OF ATOMIC CATASTROPHES

Thomas Daniell goes in search of the Temple of Atomic Catastrophes, one of the great enigmas of postwar Japanese architecture. Unbuilt, largely unexamined and never convincingly explained, this spectre continues to haunt Japan's architectural discourse, just as it possessed the architect who designed it, philosopher, calligrapher, mystic and loner, Sei'ichi Shirai.